Friedrich Mohr, Charles Siedhof

The Grape Vine

a practically scientific treatise on its management, explained from his own

experiences and researches

Friedrich Mohr, Charles Siedhof

The Grape Vine
a practically scientific treatise on its management, explained from his own experiences and researches

ISBN/EAN: 9783337082925

Printed in Europe, USA, Canada, Australia, Japan

Cover: Foto ©Andreas Hilbeck / pixelio.de

More available books at **www.hansebooks.com**

THE GRAPE VINE.

A PRACTICALLY SCIENTIFIC TREATISE ON

ITS MANAGEMENT.

EXPLAINED FROM HIS OWN EXPERIENCES AND RESEARCHES, IN A THOROUGH
AND INTELLIGIBLE MANNER, FOR VINEYARDISTS AND AMATEURS IN
GARDEN AND VINE CULTURE,

BY

FREDERICK MOHR,
DOCTOR OF PHILOSOPHY AND MEDICINE, ETC.

TRANSLATED FROM THE GERMAN, AND ACCOMPANIED WITH HINTS ON THE
PROPAGATION AND GENERAL TREATMENT OF AMERICAN VARIETIES,

BY

HORTICOLA.

.

NEW-YORK:

ORANGE JUDD & COMPANY.

41 PARK ROW.

LOVEJOY & SON,
ELECTROTYPERS AND STEREOTYPERS,
15 Vandewater street N. Y.

PREFACE OF THE AUTHOR.

To popularize the results of modern science concerning the cultivation of the grape-vine, is the object which I desire to accomplish by publishing this work. For this purpose the subject required to be reached from two directions—the earnest study of the sciences, and the practical cultivation of the vine. Progress made by mere *practice*, is slow and uncertain; *science* is too far removed from life. Both must be united to produce a material benefit. In the works extant, generally but one of the two standpoints has been kept in view.

My native city is so situate that I, with one hand, can dip the water of the Rhine, with the other, that of the Moselle—those two rivers, on the banks of which the noblest vines are produced.

The exclusively practical works, so abundant in our literature, could not give me satisfaction. The connection of cause and effect is not clearly understood; thus the explanation could not be otherwise than erroneous. What mere practice could effect, has been done long ago; without the guidance of science, improvement had become impossible.

I have cultivated the vine practically, following *Kecht*, and I have reason to boast of my success. *Kecht's* ar-

3

.

rangement, however, and his manner of treating the subject leave much to be desired. He distinguishes in a
vine eleven different things, some of which are the natural
products of the vine, viz.: *shoots* and *tendrils*; others are
the products of the hand of man, viz.: *spurs* and *arms*.
This causes confusion.

The explanation of the growth of the vine, as well as its
anatomy, as given in this book, is entirely new. The
chapter on manuring has assumed a form altogether different from that in other books. It was all-important to
elucidate fully the causes for pruning, and to show why it
has to be performed in the manner described, and in no
other, because, without this example, custom and authority
cannot be supplanted.

PREFACE OF THE TRANSLATOR.

The translation of the treatise which we offer to the American public, is the first part of Dr. *Frederic Mohr's* work *On the Treatment of the Grape-vine and on Wine-making* (*Der Weinstock und der Wein.*) The author is one of the greatest chemists of the age. That *Justus Liebeg* is one of his intimate personal friends, is well known, and evident from the fact that he wrote the second part of Dr. Mohr's standard work on Chemical Analysis by Measure (*die Titrir Methode*), detailing the analysis of soils. It has not often been the case that scientific qualifications and practical skill have been so happily united as we admire them in Dr. Mohr, whose preface explains his standpoint as well as the object he seeks to accomplish, that is, the explanation and practical application to viticulture of the results of modern science. His book does not interfere with any work extant; it is rather a complement to all of them, as its object is to explain the principles of viticulture, and describes only a few methods of training for the sake of illustration. In Germany, it is considered as the best and most thorough book on the Culture of the Grape vine among their many works on the same subject. In a recent letter to me, Dr. Edw. Lucas, the great Pomologist, whom I had requested to give me a list of

5

the best books on viticulture, says: "Dr. Mohr's book is
the most thorough and best of all." It does not need my
praise; it will speak for itself.

Although the second part of the original *On Wine-
making* is as important as the first, yet I concluded to
separate the two, as there are many more persons interested in the cultivation of the vine than in making wine.
I shall, however, commence the translation of the second
part very soon.

In regard to the hints on the propagation and the general treatment of American varieties which I have added,
I hope to meet the wants of many readers. Being very
far from assuming the task of giving instruction, I wish
only to encourage such as may feel disposed to devote
part of their leisure hours to a branch of horticulture
which is as pleasant as it is useful.

I cannot let this occasion pass, without expressing my
admiration of the great zeal and enthusiasm with which
viticulture is pursued in this country at present. The
names of *Longworth* and *Underhill* will, in the history of
American Grape Culture, never be forgotten. But it is
chiefly due to the indefatigable exertions of Dr. *C. W.
Grant*, of Iona, that, especially at the East, the love for
viticulture was awakened, and is now so irresistibly spreading. The labors of the editors of the Horticultural Magazines, Messrs. Mead, Woodward, Meehan, Hovey and
Tilton, and those of the editors of the Agricultural Peri-
odicals, such as the *American Agriculturist*, the *Country
Gentleman*, and others, can not be too highly appreciated.
Dr. Grant's Illustrated Catalogues and *Manual of
Grape Culture*, have had the most happy influence on
spreading sound views on the treatment of the grape
among large numbers of people.

Andrew S. Fuller's Grape Culturist appeared at the
right time. It is a full, clear exposition of all that is,
needed for practical success. The author treats the sub-

ject in so lucid and comprehensive a manner, that his book
will be used for a long time to come. The works of
Ernst, Muench, Strong, Husmann, and others, will continue
doing good wherever they are known.

I have abstained from interrupting Dr. Mohr's text by
inserting remarks except in one or two places; the chapter
on mildew I shortened, omitting what relates to arrangements to be made in towns and villages against the
Oïdium, because those arrangements are utterly impracticable in this country.

I am in the habit of contributing occasionally some
trifles to several of our Horticultural magazines under the
nom-de-plume *Horticola*. They have been received by the
horticultural public in the spirit in which I wrote them;
to collect and establish *facts*, is the only aim I have in
view. I hope some may profit by my little success, and
be saved from disappointment by my failures; for I state
both, frankly and candidly. In order not to mislead any
body that knows me under my nom-de-plume, I retain it
on the title of this translation. The praise this little book
merits, belongs to Dr. Mohr; all I claim for my hints is
the indulgence of the readers.

CHARLES SIEDHOF,
Weehawken, N. J.

CONTENTS.

8

THE GRAPE VINE.

The grape vine is, among the plants, what the horse is among animals,—one of the most precious boons nature has given to man. It follows him to climates of a very different character, and admirably rewards him for all the trouble devoted to it. As in the horse, everything in the grape vine is beautiful and noble. The delicately shaped leaves, the fragrant blossoms, the delicious grapes, extend their development over the whole year, except during the severe months of winter, and require uninterrupted and careful treatment by the hand of man. The grape vine grows on the rocky hill, and in the fertile garden, trails on the ground and climbs to the roofs of houses. By training it may be kept as a small shrub, or made to cover a surface of a thousand square feet.

The grape vine changes its character, and adapts itself in a wonderful manner to every country, that affords it the necessary warmth. With facility it produces, in the hand of man, new varieties, which conform themselves to all circumstances. The difference in the varieties is as great as in the various races of dogs. The berry varies in size from that of a large pea to that of a cherry; its color is green, yellow, flesh color, red, blue, and black. Sweetness and acidity are mixed in the most varying proportions; its aroma is unsurpassed.

The grape is decidedly the most noble of fruits; it is sweeter than any other, and the admixture of a little acid

9   1*   •

renders it exceedingly delicious. The liquid contents of the grape elevates it above the hard apple. It is the only fruit of our climate which is drunk, rather than eaten. Finally, the fermented juice of the grape, the wine, prolongs the time of the enjoyment of it for a series of years. For these reasons, the treatment of the grape vine and of wine have frequently been the object of human care, and even the poets have not felt ashamed to be inspired by it.

The grape vine is a plant belonging to temperate climates. It is found on the continent within a zone, the northern border of which extends from the British Channel through Northern Germany, to the north of the Black and the Caspian Seas to China; its southern border is the coast of Northern Africa to Egypt, where the line bends from Suez to the point of the Persian Gulf, not touching the sea coast any more. It does not grow in Arabia and Hindoostan.

The northern border of the vine region commences at the mouth of the Loire, (47½° N. L.) Receding from the Ocean, it suddenly bends northward, and extends north of Paris to 50° N. L.; it enters Belgium between Maestricht and Liege, and touches near Bonn, at the fifty-first degree of N. L.

The line runs along the banks of the Rhine to Mayence, where it passes into the valley of the Maine. Thence it passes through Thuringia, touching the Elbe near Meissen. It reaches Greenberg, extending through Guben to Lausatia, where it reaches the fifty-second degree of N. L. Thence the line bends abruptly towards the south, and includes Bohemia. The borders of the wine region do not coincide with certain isothermal lines, so that not all countries of a certain average warmth are fit for the cultivation of the vine. It requires a long, warm summer, and is able to bear a considerable degree of cold in the winter. Although the winters of England are very mild, yet the grape vine does not flourish there, because the summers are not warm enough. The hard frozen soil at Tokay, in Hungaria, does not prevent the production of wine of the greatest excellence. A sea climate is favorable to viticulture only in lower latitudes; in Germany, it extends nearly two degrees further north than in France, situated nearer to the Ocean. Bordeaux, on the Atlantic Ocean, produces wines similar to those produced in Burgundy, which is considerably more northward, but inland.

There are, without those borders, here and there certain places where the vine grows, yet it is, within them, confined to certain favorable localities and cannot be grown everywhere. It is remarkable that the most delicious and precious wines are produced almost exclusively near the northern border of its cultivation. The noble Ahrbleichert, and the Walporzheimer, which rivals the wine of Bordeaux and Burgundy, grow immediately on the northern border of viticulture. Only a few miles further north, the cultivation of the vine in vineyards ceases entirely, and the vine is only found growing on trellises and houses. The Johannisberg, Ruedesheim, Steinberg and Rauenthal, are grown on the northern border of viticulture in the Rhinegau, from east to west. Only a few hundred paces to the north, there are the Westerwald and the Taunus.

The true poetry of wine, its beautiful fragrance, called the bouquet of the wine, is the exclusive property of the northern regions. The wines of the south, however rich in alcohol and sugar, are entirely destitute of that bouquet; or they have a common odor, like Port, Madeira, Xeres, and Malaga, without any peculiarity. The difference, produced by localities and years, disappears in the wines of those regions entirely, but it may be distinguished in those of northern regions with great accuracy.

Viticulture has also its history; it is linked with that of man. The vine has perished in regions that are no longer inhabited; and where it, at present, grows wild, there it was not originally at home.

The Pramucic and Marœotic wine is only known from Homer; and such as was given by Ulysses to the Cyclopes, has disappeared. (*Vide* Homer's Odysea, IX, 208). Wines, which can bear that poetical dilution, are unknown to us. Also the *Vinum Cœcubum, Massicum* and *Falernum*, of Horace, have disappeared from causes which we shall learn afterwards.

DEVELOPMENT AND STRUCTURE OF THE VINE.

In order to understand the rules for the pruning and the treatment of the vine, it is necessary to study the very simple structure of that plant.

Without this knowledge, all practical rules appear entirely arbitrary; their necessity can not be understood, nor can they be carried out with the proper enthusiasm. The rules for the management of the vine, derived from a long experience, are based on its peculiar structure, and are, as soon as that is known, intelligible in themselves. In particular cases, where horticultural books fail us, we are able to infer the true treatment of the vine from the knowledge of its structure. We, therefore, premise an accurate explanation of the structure of the vine in a manner not before attempted; then the practical instruction will follow.

THE NODE.

That organ, by the repetition of which the vine is constructed, is the *node* in the branch. If we look at a fresh shoot of a vine, we see that it has nodes, (or joints,) from three to five inches distant from each other, and at these places all other organs of the vine are put forth nearly at the same level. These nodes are repeated on a shoot in a manner perfectly alike, only the organs grow in a reversed position of right and left in each following node.

We will now carefully examine the node. We take a branch which grew from an eye in the last spring, and is, in the course of the summer, still green. Fig. 1, represents such a node. Where the swelling has not quite reached its greatest dimensions, there is, in the branch, a joint.

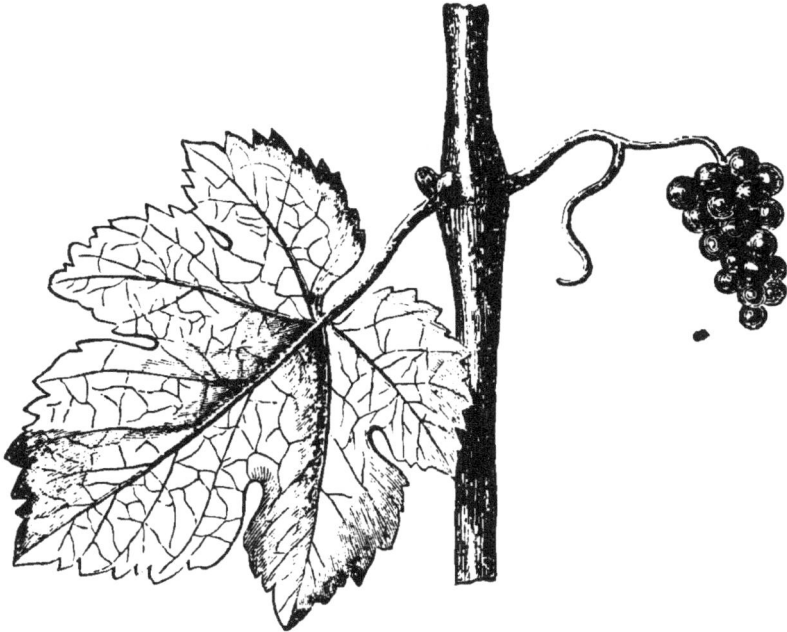

Fig. 1.—THE NODE.

A young branch breaks easily in this place when bent towards one side. On the lower side there is either nothing or only the leaf—*all protruding organs grow on the upper part.* This structure shows that the wood fibers do not, as yet, run through. While a branch cannot be broken off smoothly in any other place, it is there very brittle. In the course of time this joint disappears; the fibers run through, and in the latter part of the summer a node cannot be broken off in this place. Immediately above the place where it is broken, there is on one side, 1st, a *leaf,* the footstalk of which commences with a protuberance. The leaf itself is connected with the branch by

means of a joint. It is easier to break it off in this place
than in any other, without protruding filaments. The
joint does not grow over, and in the fall the leaf separates
at this point.

In the axil of the leaf, 2nd, *one or two unequally large
buds* grow, from which the so-called laterals proceed.
Generally only one lateral grows; should there be double
buds, the weaker ones must always be destroyed. By the
side of the lateral a new eye, the so-called dormant bud,
forms in the course of the summer. It is intended to remain during the winter on the vine, and to furnish, in the
next spring, a green branch. On carefully examining those
buds, we find that on two nodes succeeding each other,
the bud is in one of them to the right of the lateral, and
in the other to the left of it. The branch growing from
the bud is attached to the main cane by means of a joint,
and can, as long as it is young, be easily broken off in
this place. In the latter part. of the summer, however,
the wood fibers grow through, and the secondary branch
cannot then be broken off at the joint.

On the opposite side of the leaf and bud, but at the
same level with them, there is, 3d, a *tendril* or a *cluster*, but
without a joint. The fibers run through from the very
beginning, there is no articulation, and the tendril or
the cluster cannot be broken off at the place of its origin.
The tendril, or the peduncle of the cluster, dries up in the
fall, but never drops; they are separated from the cane in
the following year by motion and wind, because they are
brittle. Tendril and cluster are identical organs. There
are tendrils with some few berries on them, and clusters
with a piece of a tendril without berries. Tendril and
cluster never grow by the side of each other. One proof
of their identity is to be found in the fact that they grow
from the cane without a joint, and that they dry up in the
fall, and do not drop.

If there are tendrils on two successive nodes, the third

node is always without them, and the place of the node opposite the leaf, and the bud presents a roundish protuberance without any branch. A node destitute of tendrils is succeeded by two nodes with tendrils, and so in regular order to the end of the branch.

As tendril and cluster are identical organs, it follows that three successive nodes never bear clusters; if more than two clusters proceed from one bud, then the third and fourth clusters are separated from the first and second by a node destitute of tendrils.

Recapitulating briefly, we find that the organs on a node are distinguished by the following peculiarities:

1. The leaf is connected with the branch by a joint, through which no fibers grow, but from which it drops of itself.

2. The bud is connected with the branch by a joint, through which the fibers grow and harden. It does not drop.

3. The tendril or cluster is connected with the branch without a joint. The place of the connection dries up, and it does not drop of itself.

THE BRANCH.

The branch originates in the repetition of the nodes. The distance of two nodes from each other is smaller on the lower part of the cane, greater on the upper part, generally from three to five inches, but oftentimes more, or less. On each of the succeeding nodes the organs are found alternating with the preceding and following. In the place where there is a leaf on one node there is a tendril, or a bunch in the preceding and following one.

The number of the nodes on a branch is very large, commonly from 25 to 30. I have counted sometimes as many as 83 on strong growing varieties. The number is, properly speaking, unlimited, for in the fall the growth of

the branch terminates, as is shown in figure 2, exactly
with the same fan-like structure, with which it commenced
in the spring.

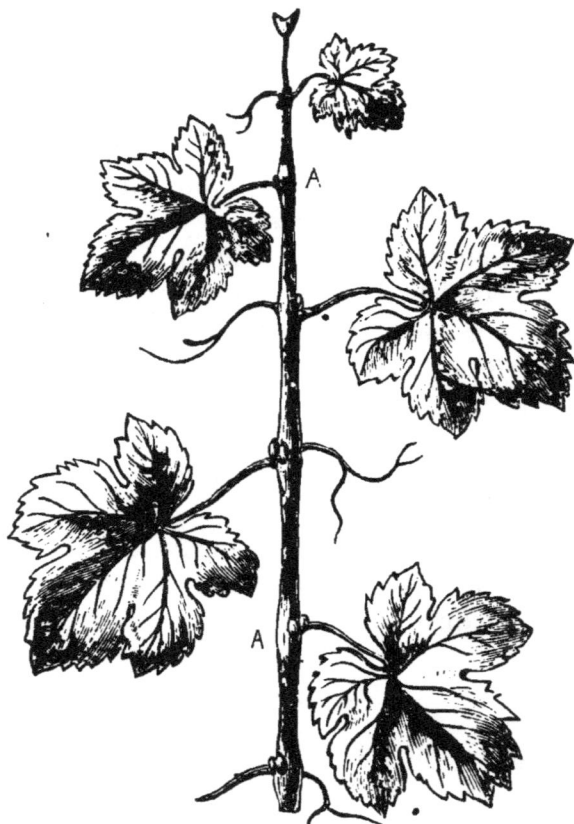

Fig. 2.—THE BRANCH.

In this lie enclosed innumerable nodes, the development
of which is only prevented by the ending of the season
of growth, and the exhausted vigor of the plant. In a
warm summer and climate, therefore, many more nodes
will grow than in a cold one.

On a shoot grown in the spring, there is only a limited
number of blossoms or bunches. They are produced only
on the lower part of the green shoot, almost without any

regularity. The shoot commences with three or four nodes, which are either without blossoms or have only small tendrils; then two clusters follow; then a node. without a tendril, (as in fig. 2); then the third cluster; then again tendrils, which grow the larger the nearer they are to the top of the shoot.

The number of clusters on a green shoot depends on the variety of the vine. The rule is *two clusters from one bud*, sometimes from three to five; I have never seen more than five clusters. If the latter part of the winter and the forepart of spring are warm, oftentimes three clusters grow from one bud, even if the variety bears generally but two. If we recollect that an eye produces, on the average, three bunches, but that the shoot may produce from thirty to seventy nodes, it is obvious that a grape vine can produce a large quantity of wood and leaves which are useless for the production of grapes. The clusters grow especially from the lowermost nodes. The longest tendrils are found on the uppermost nodes, where the plant needs the most support. If a tendril touches a solid body only slightly, it bends towards it, coils several times around it, and holds to it firmly. The cause of this must lie in the structure of the tendril, which is different from all other parts of the vine, in the fact that it dries up in the fall without dropping. The tendrils seem to be endowed with vision, as it were, because they grow towards any solid body near them.

The eyes of the shoots are all of the same nature. *There are neither wood nor fruit buds exclusively.* After an unfavorable, cold season, the eyes show in the next spring no blossoms; after a very warm season, they nearly all produce blossoms. This proves that the blossoms are a higher development of the bud, because greater heat was necessary for it. The blossoms are, therefore, always formed in the preceding year, and they appear in the following, however unfavorable the weather may be. Thus two years are required for the production of a heavy crop of grapes.

At the base of the leaves on the green shoot, there always grow two eyes. One of them pushes during the summer, and forms what is called the *lateral.* It has been already mentioned that, alternately, the right and the left eye push or remain dormant on two successive nodes. This lateral has all the organs like every other shoot, and a whole vine may be grown from each of them. Generally, the word *lateral* is believed to convey the meaning of a superfluous organ, which nature has carelessly produced. This view is entirely erroneous, and experiments will prove *that the lateral is capable of producing as heavy crops as the most vigorous cane.* If a lateral is broken off, the other eye pushes, and a new eye commences to be formed. If the second lateral is also broken off, the new eye pushes, and another dormant eye is formed. This may be repeated six or seven times during a warm summer.

If, on the contrary, the first lateral is not removed, the dormant eye does not push, and it is changed, in the course of the summer, into a fruit bud for the next year. Should, however, the last formed eye not have originated until midsummer, it cannot be so developed that it becomes a fruit bud, and it produces in the next year nothing but leaves and wood.

Hence it follows that, if we wish a certain eye to become a fruit bud for the next year, we must *not* remove the lateral growing beside it. If the laterals, in a warm summer, are broken off, and the dormant eye pushes, it often shows blossoms in August, which cannot mature their fruit on account of the season being so far advanced. This shows conclusively that the formation of blossom buds takes place in the course of the summer preceding that of the production of fruit. In the year 1858, which was unusually warm, the fruit of the second blossoms also matured, so that two crops, only a month distant from each other, were obtained from Burgundy vines. The second crop was less abundant, and not so good as the first.

When a person, without any knowledge of the management of the vine, breaks off the end of the shoot without any definite plan, in order to diminish the quantity of the foliage, not unfrequently blossoms appear a fortnight after that operation. The eyes which are forced in this way to produce blossoms are those that ought to have been developed in the following year. The eyes formed afterwards cannot mature their blossoms on account of the lateness of the season in which they are formed.

It is absolutely necessary to understand fully this mode of the growth of the vine, because all the rules for growing it, so as to obtain the largest quantity of fruit in a given place, are based on it.

Towards the close of the season, the following changes take place in the shoots that have grown from an eye :

1. The leaf turns yellow, and drops from the joint of itself.

2. The peduncle, or the tendril corresponding to it, dries up, but does not drop of itself.

Fig. 3.—THE NODE IN AUTUMN.

3. The green shoot is changed into wood and remains permanent, the joints becoming united with the shoot by the two growing together.

4. The green color of the shoot is turned brown. The wood matures.

5. The eye remains dormant until the following spring. The new branch has now the form of figure 3.

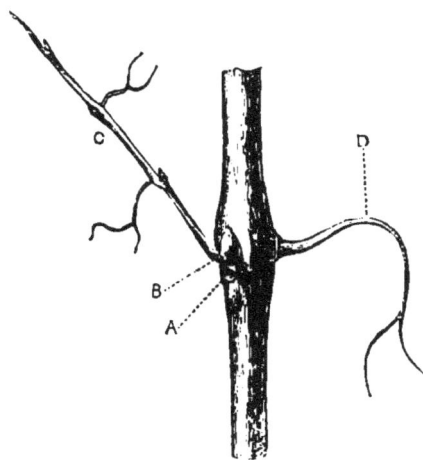

At *A*, below the eye, the place is visible where the foot stalk of the leaf was attached; above, there is the eye, *B*, which is going to push in the following year, and to bear fruit. A second eye does not exist during the winter; it is developed in the next spring. Beside the eye, *B*, the lateral, *C*, is visible. It is to be removed entirely in the fall. On the opposite side there is the tendril, *D*, or the peduncle of the bunch, dried up.

The first period of the life of the shoot terminates by changing its succulent nature into wood. In the first year it bears clusters attached to it with their peduncles; in the next year no cluster grows immediately on it, but on the green shoot which pushes from the eye perfected in the preceding year. Consequently the shoot bears clusters only once in its life; in the next year they appear on the shoot from the eye; in the third year on the shoot that grows from the shoot; in the fourth year on the shoot of the shoot which grows from the shoot, and so on, ad infinitum.

It is now necessary to introduce, instead of the generally used expression *branch*, those terms which are made use of in viticulture.

As soon as the green shoot has changed its color and turned brown, and the clusters growing immediately from it have been harvested, it receives the name of *cane*; it retains this name a whole year, until the clusters have been gathered from its side branches, when it becomes part of the *stem*.

During the time the cane was green it was called a *shoot*.

We distinguish, therefore, in a grape vine, the following three parts, viz. :

1. The *shoot*, of green color, grown in this year from the eye, bearing the grapes immediately on the peduncle. Its course of life lasts from May until October, or half a year; it was an eye from October until May, also half a year.

2. The *cane*, of brown color, and of smooth bark, bearing the clusters on a side branch, the shoot. Its course of life is from October to October, or a year.

3. The *stem*, of black color, the bark separating from it, bearing the clusters with the shoot on the cane. Its course of life embraces the age of the grape vine, of from 800 to 1000 years.

The grape vine, therefore, is progressing regularly ; the shoot is changed to a cane, and the cane to a stem. The stem enlarges more and more as the canes of the preceding year are added to it. The necessary consequence of this process is that the stem, which does not bear grapes, increases more and more in extent, and that the clusters cannot grow but on the extreme ends of the stem, because they are the product of the green shoots proceeding from the eye. It follows from these facts that we have to resort to a method to compel the vine to produce new canes over its whole extent, lest the greater part of the available space would be occupied by the never-bearing stem. This method consists in pruning or training, that is, an intentional and artificial removal of some parts, to compel others near them to push.

Pruning the grape vine has, from time immemorial, been considered necessary in its cultivation, although the true connection between cause and effect has not been sufficiently well understood. The vine, however, is capable of so much development that even faulty pruning always accomplishes a part of its object. Before we proceed to show practically the true way of pruning, we must study the reasons which render it efficient.

THE REASONS FOR PRUNING.

In the course of the year the movement of the sap in the grape vine is subject to great differences. In the spring, when the temperature rises, the sap begins to rise also. The eyes swell and produce green shoots. If a cane is cut, drops of water flow out—it bleeds. The power with which the vine forces the sap upwards is so great that we shall devote to it a particular chapter further on. In no plant is the water flowing out so copious as in the vine. If we look at a growing grape vine attentively, we observe that the development of the eyes is the greater the nearer they are to the top of it. The length and size of the shoot increase toward the top of the canes, and decrease toward the stem. We do not know the cause of the movement of the sap; we cannot explain it as satisfactorily as we can the cause of the movement of the blood in the animals, in which it originates from the contraction of the heart.

We infer from the fact that the development of the eyes increases toward the top, that the cause of the movement of the sap is active over the whole length of the cane. This violent and enormous movement of the sap lasts but a short time, and soon ceases entirely, so that a cane may be cut, and not lose a single drop of sap. If we cut off the uppermost node of a cane, the node preceding it, being now the uppermost, shows a powerful growth; if we cut off a longer piece of cane, the most vigorous growth always takes place at the then uppermost node. From this fact arises the possibility of inducing development on any place by cutting above it. The pushing sap, not any more required for the nourishment of the portions cut off, is compelled to contribute to the growth of the eyes below the cut.

We have seen in the above, that if we remove a green shoot, the dormant eye beside it pushes immediately. This is a fact similar to that explained. If we cut back to the stem, so that no canes are left on a part of the stem, the rising sap causes the stem to produce new eyes on its nodes. As these did not exist in the spring, they are not sufficiently developed to produce flowers; the eyes, therefore, pushing from the stem, are necessarily wood eyes, but they are capable of producing fruit eyes during the summer. This fact enables us to shorten the stem and to make it produce canes. We cut it off, therefore, in a certain place, so that nodes are left below it. If the wood eyes which are then formed, and have pushed, are permitted to grow undisturbed, they can bear fruit the next year. The powerful development of the stem, described in the above, which all canes a year old have also, compels us to keep the enlargement of the stem within bounds, and to force, by pruning, the nodes below to produce shoots and canes.

The natural development of a cane which is permitted to grow undisturbed, and without any check, has the following result:

Supposing we have a cane of ten nodes, ten shoots will grow in the spring, each of which may bear three clusters, i. e., thirty clusters on the whole. If all the shoots are permitted to grow, each may have produced in the fall ten nodes, that is, a hundred nodes on the shoots which will became canes in the fall, and these may bear in the following year three hundred bunches. In the third year, the hundred nodes would produce a thousand eyes, and would consequently bear three thousand bunches. Nature has circumscribed such a development, which is only imaginary; for the root would hardly be able to furnish, in the three succeeding years, food for the three hundred, certainly not for the three thousand bunches. It is evident, at all events, that a vine, not restrained in its growth, would spread so enormously that any given place would become too small; the stem would, at least every year, increase in its height as much as one node is distant from the other. This is plain from figure 4, in which only the lowest shoots on each cane are shown. The cane, 1, which grows immediately from the stem, would, after the lapse of a year, become a part of the stem. After two years more the cane

2, after three years the cane 3, and so on, so that after
five years the stem would reach to nine. It is a most favorable circumstance that we have chosen every year the

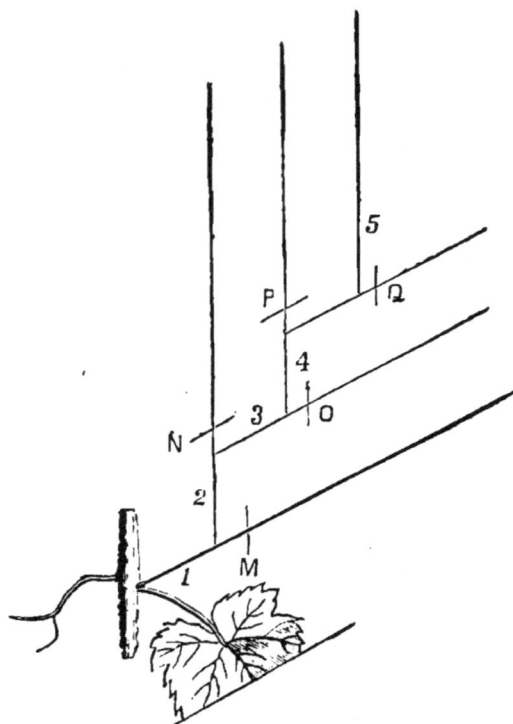

Fig. 4.—PLAN OF GROWTH.

lowermost shoot to bear next year. Should it be necessary to choose a cane growing higher up, the stem ·would
lengthen in height much more rapidly. The stem increases
every year one node in height.

If we further assume that there, where the cane, 1, bears
fruit this year, is room only for one cane, the existing
space being occupied exactly in the same manner, we see
the necessity of cutting off, in the fall, the cane, 1, above
its lowermost eye, that is, at *M*, after it has borne fruit.
In the following year the shoot, 2, pushes and bears fruit.
After the expiration of the second year it must be cut at

N. Now the shoot, 3, pushes, which must be cut at *O* after the third year; in like manner the shoot, 4, grows in the fourth year, and must be cut at *P;* the shoot, 5, at *Q,* and so forth.

This is the foundation of the pruning of the vine, according to which the stem increases one node in each year, and only one cane is expected to grow in the place of another cane removed.

After a series of years the stem has necessarily increased in height, and must be shortened. The method to accomplish this object will be explained in that part of the work which treats of pruning practically applied.

THE PRUNING OF THE GRAPE VINE.

The necessity of pruning has been explained in the preceding chapter. We wish now to show the practical application of it in a vine fully grown, and occupying the whole space allotted to it. This is the most frequent of all cases, because it takes only a few years to train a vine; it will last, when properly managed, for centuries. The propagation and management of young vines will be treated of in another place.

There is a classical work on the pruning of the vine by J. S. Kecht, the seventh edition of which was issued in 1853. As Kecht's method is based on the nature of the vine itself, no improvement on it has been made in any of the more recent horticultural books. If we follow his directions as laid down in the book, we are easily convinced of the correctness of his teachings, and success is certain. The experience of many years has proved the advantages derived from Kecht's method.

In pruning a grape vine, we wish to accomplish two object, viz. :

1. To obtain for the current year as much fruit as possible.

2

2. To produce vigorous canes for bearing the next year.

The first pruning of the vine ought to be done in the fall, commencing in the middle of November, after the fall of the leaf; it may be continued during the winter when the weather is favorable. The advantages of fall pruning are very great. It is easier to manage a pruned vine during the winter than an unpruned one ; no sap is lost in the next spring by bleeding; the pieces cut off can be buried in a compost heap and converted into manure.

The pruning of the vine is modified by the system of training preferred. By this we understand the manner in which the vine is to be extended. The vine is either trained on walls, (trellis,) or on poles, (common vineyard training,) or on wires, which may be stretched high or low.

For each of these modes of training, the pruning is a little different, but not much, as the principle remains the same.

TRAINING ON TRELLISES.

In order to prune a grape vine, trained to a trellis, it is necessary to loosen the vine by cutting the osiers, or other material with which it was tied, either with a knife or garden shears. Then the canes for bearing must be selected, and also those which are to be spurred for the production of new canes. The strongest are chosen for bearing ; they must be entirely brown, having been changed from shoots to canes during the summer and fall just passed. Their tops are generally not ripened, and are consequently green. The green part must be entirely cut away, because it would be killed in the winter. The cane is so much shortened that it reaches, in the position in which it is to be tied, about one-third to the top of the whole trellis. One-third must remain unoccupied, because it is required for tying the shoot to it that pushes from the last eye of the cane. If we suppose that the trellis is from six to seven feet high, and that six feet of its length on each side is to be occupied by the vine, the canes in the middle are pruned to the length of four feet, those on each side spreading, in the shape of a fan, to the length of five or six feet. Therefore from eight to fourteen buds will remain on each cane, promising an abundant crop. Such canes are to be preferred as grow lowest on the stem. *No old wood ought to be found beyond the middle of the height of the trellis.* After the selection and pruning of the canes, the stem, (that is, the cane which bore fruit in the preceding summer and fall,) is cut off immediately above the place where the new canes grow; the canes themselves must be cut off an inch above the bud, as, if cut close, this would be apt to dry up.

It is true that a cane having from ten to fourteen buds can bear from twenty to thirty clusters; yet it is not probable that it will make strong shoots. To remedy this, some weaker canes are selected in the fall for the production of bearing canes, by cutting them back to two buds each. A cane so pruned is called a *spur.*

This spur receives, when the vine grows, as much sap as a cane having ten or twelve buds; but as this sap serves for the development and pushing of only two buds, the shoots proceeding from them are very vigorous and of strong growth. Each of the two shoots may bear from four to six clusters, yet the spur is not intended for bearing. If the blossoms on them are removed, the cane growing from the spur will be so much the stronger. Should both buds of the spur be equally vigorous and strong, they may be left; but if they are feeble, one is to be removed, which makes the remaining shoot very much stronger. *The place for the spurs ought to be as low as possible on the stem,* so that the canes proceeding from them may bear fruit along the whole height of the trellis.

Also wood buds, pushing from the old wood, may be cut to spurs in the fall. • *The shoots pushing from the spurs in the following spring must not be interfered with;*

they must be permitted to grow undisturbed. Also, all weaker canes not intended for bearing, and growing very low on the stem, must be cut back to spurs of two buds each. Should there be too many shoots in the next year to serve as canes, some of them are pinched in, and may be permitted to bear fruit.

A little higher up on the stem, some canes are pruned to four or five eyes. Canes so pruned are called *long spurs.* They bear fruit, but not so much as the canes, and are therefore able to produce stronger canes. In this way the vine is compelled to produce strong bearing canes all over, which is the condition of fruitfulness every year. So the stem is also kept within certain bounds. If these precautionary measures are neglected, the grape vine may bear for one year a large quantity of fruit; the next year there will be many, but feeble, canes, all growing high up on the stem. The height of the stem will have considerably increased, and will show no fruit below.

Should the trellis be much higher than twelve or sixteen feet, as on walls of houses or barns, it is impossible to reach this height with a single cane. In this case a part of the stem is carried up to half the height of the trellis, and canes are grown from it to cover the upper part of the trellis; the lower part is covered with canes proceeding, near the bottom, from side branches of the stem, which are then treated exactly as described above. It is almost impossible to keep vines, trained on such trellises, in order, because it is impracticable, by means of a ladder, to perform the labor needed by the vine.

[It is a much better plan to plant more than one vine, when, for instance, the first is trained low, the second high, the third low again, and so on alternately.—*Remark of the Translator.*]

The pruning of a vine trained to a post is much simpler. The best developed canes are pruned to eight or ten buds, and also some of the lower ones to spurs. The manner of

tying the canes, either more horizontally, or at certain
angles to the horizon, as well as the length to which they
are pruned, varies very much in all regions where vines are
grown. None of those methods can be considered as absolutely the best ; for each of them is recommended as the
best in the region where it is practised. Some do not
wish to grow many clusters, in order to obtain fruit of the
highest character; others prune their canes long, to obtain
a large number of bunches. Aside from the different
opinions and views of the people, the character of the soil
exerts so powerful an influence that the little changes de-
manded by each locality are gradually understood by those
inhabitants of it who cultivate the vine. The principles
of pruning are the same for every mode of training : *the
most beautiful and strongest canes are selected for bearing, while the weaker canes are, by short pruning, forced
to produce strong shoots.*

If, however, in consequence of an unfavorable spring,
no blossoms appear, or if they have perished by late frosts,
rains and other accidents, the first of the ends in grape
culture, namely, to grow clusters for the current, and canes
for the following year, cannot be accomplished, so that the
second must be kept in view exclusively. In this case the
canes that had been grown for fruiting are pruned back
to two eyes, and the shoots proceeding from them are permitted to grow undisturbed. In like manner, all shoots
of a cane without fruit may be removed, so that only one
leaf near the bud remains. The bunches, as well as the
shoots intended for canes, will in this way be much better
developed. *There exists a mutual action and re-action
between the canes and the leaf, and the root and the stem.*
A strong root is able to produce many canes and rich foliage, which latter tends in its turn to enlarge the stem
and the root. All carbonaceous formations in the vine, as
well as in every other plant, are the result of the fact that
the leaves, under the influence of heat and light, decom-

pose carbonic acid, set oxygen free, and deposit carbon in connection with the elements of the water for the production of organic matter in the vine.

The so-called hydrates of carbon are grape sugar, starch, wood fibre, and also the other formations like tartaric acid; the green of the leaves, oil, and so forth, originate under the same conditions.

If there are many leaves on the vine, large quantities of oxygen are given off to the air, and so corresponding quantities of grape sugar and wood fibre are formed. Hence it follows that the foliage must be ample to develop many bunches, the number of which is different every year; *the foliage is needed to nourish the fruit, and to render it sweet.* If, for the sake of experiment, all the leaves of a cane are removed, the berries and clusters growing on it remain small, sour and hard, and the wood does not ripen. Rich foliage tends to ripen the fruit as well as the wood.

The growth of the wood and of the root depends, therefore, chiefly on the quantity of the leaves, especially when the leaves have not to furnish nourishment. *From this circumstance results the practical rule not to remove any leaves, if we wish to make the vine grow strong. Although the richness and sweetness of the fruit depend on the foliage, yet this is also owing to the extent and activity of the root.* A young vine, with a comparatively small and weak root, can furnish sap for a small number of clusters only, even if all the leaves remain on it. The extent and power of the root increases every year, so that the vine will bear and ripen larger quantities of clusters annually. If the proportion of the root, the foliage and the fruit be right, a large and old vine will bear several thousand of clusters, which will be as mature and sweet as twelve or twenty would be on a small vine, the root of which is yet feeble.

The nourishment is taken by the root and conducted to the plant. It is elaborated in the leaf, where oxygen is

eliminated, and where the inorganic carbonic acid is converted into an organic compound; then the nourishment is
deposited and collected in the berry. The true growth of
the vine lies, therefore, in the surface of the leaves dis-
played in the sunlight, while the clusters on a vine which
is growing naturally are protected from the direct rays of
the sun.

It is sufficient when the sun shines on the leaves, and
the clusters are growing in diffused light. This is the
true and natural condition. It is now not difficult to understand how great a mistake is made when the leaf, growing near a cluster, is removed for the purpose of admit-
ting the rays of the sun directly to the cluster. No sugar
can be formed in the berry, because no oxygen can be
eliminated by it; the berry only collects the sugar, or it
prepares it from an organic substance formed by the leaf.
The berry is apt to be injured by the direct rays of the
sun during the hot days of summer, (sunstroke).

The development of the vine may, therefore, take place
within limits that may either be very small or very large.
In the steep vineyards of the Moselle, where vegetable
mould and loam are wanting, so that frequently the necessary soil must be carried up in baskets from the valley, a
vine cannot grow to a large extent.

The canes are as thin as a lead pencil; the stem is as
thick as a finger; the clusters are few, but excellent, provided there is the right proportion between the foliage and
the fruit. The circumstance that the vines are planted
very near each other, and that the soil is very shallow,
prevents the extension of the root, so that the whole plant
is crippled during its term of life. It cannot, however,
be otherwise under the existing circumstances.

A vine, growing in rich garden soil, produces canes
twenty feet long, studded with from sixty to eighty nodes
each. A vine, four years old, can, in such soil, bear four
hundred clusters. In the year 1826, Kecht counted on a

vine of the Fruch-Leipziger 4,500 clusters; in other years,
generally from two to three thousand. This was at Berlin,
the capital of Prussia. The celebrated Hampton Court
vine, near London, planted by Cardinal Wolsey, and still
growing in a large glass house, bears every year more than
a thousand excellent clusters.

TREATMENT OF THE VINE IN THE SUMMER.

When the vine is pruned before winter, it is not tied,
but permitted to swing in the air, or to lie on the ground.
It suffers less from the cold by being moved by the air,
than when it is fixed to a certain place where it must lose
a great deal of heat by radiation. It is a well known fact
that solid bodies lose, in clear nights, much more than
aeriform bodies; consequently the vine will be colder by
radiation than the surrounding air. If it moves freely in
the air, it comes constantly into contact with new strata
of air which are warmer than itself, and is, in this way,
protected from being killed by the frost. The vine suffers
from the frost when the thermometer is about at zero,
[though many American varieties can stand much more
cold.—*Translator.*] In Western Germany, on the Rhine,
the Moselle and the Saar, the vines are left on the ground
in winter; in the east of Germany, they must be covered
with soil, to protect them against being killed by the frost.
Every one has, in this respect, to do what the climate of
the country requires.

During the whole winter, changes are constantly going
on in the vine. Should it come to a stand still, the plant
must die. These changes take place in accordance with
the warmth of the winter, so that in mild winters the
eyes begin to swell in January and February. That the
vine is dormant in winter, shows that it belongs to the temperate zone. It is not the cold which causes this dormant
condition, but the natural desire for rest, to prepare itself

for new exertions in the next year. In the island of Madeira, f. i., the vine drops its leaves in October, after it has ripened its fruit, and remains dormant during the winter months, the warmth of which is equal to that of our summers. Surrounded by evergreen·native plants, the vine is there as leafless as with us; it remains in this dormant condition for one hundred and sixty days, until it awakens in March to commence life anew.

As soon as the heavy frosts are over, which is, with us, (on the Rhine) after the middle of February, the vine may be tied to its post or trellis. Usually this is done a little later, i. e., in the course of March, and in the first part of April. As at the time of tying, some little pruning will frequently take place, it is advisable to commence it as early as possible, so that the wounds may dry up again, and may not bleed afterwards. The remaining canes are equally distributed all over the trellis, to cover the space, and are tied with osiers or bast matting. The necessary manipulations can be easily learned from any gardener or vineyardist; without this, they are so obvious in themselves that a trial will be all that is needed to understand them.

The eyes of the vines commence pushing and are developed into green shoots, on which, from the middle of April to the middle of May, the blossoms appear, but only as blossom buds. [The blossom buds are called, in German, *Scheine* or *Gescheine*, for which expressions the English language has as yet no corresponding words.—*Translator.*] We know from the process of the development of the vine, that from each eye a shoot will push, and that we need every year the same number of canes. If all the shoots should be suffered to grow, the vines would have in the next year as many canes as there were eyes in the preceding year; the vine would, in the summer, be nothing but a confused mass of wood and leaves. To prevent this, the pushing shoots are in a certain manner either *rubbed*

2*

off or *pinched.* In these operations two objects are kept
in view, viz.: to obtain the best possible fruit, and to develop only as many canes as are actually on the vine. The
honor of the discovery of the method to accomplish this is
also due to Keeht; in it, his teachings have reached their
culminating point. According to the opinion of all those
who understand viticulture, nothing that is either better,
or even as good, has been brought to light; the method is
so simple, and in accordance with the laws of nature, that
we may consider it, without hesitation, perfect.

We do not wish to grow more canes than the vine is
bearing. It follows that only one eye on each cane must
be used for a new one. *The eye to be used for a cane
must be necessarily the lowermost.* The sap has a strong
upward tendency, and causes the uppermost canes to grow
strongest; the growth of the shoots proceeding from the
higher part of the cane must, therefore, be restrained. On
them the clusters, in which the object of growing the
vine centers, are produced. The restriction of the upper
shoots must be so managed as to conduce to the best
growth of the clusters. The two following rules unite
everything that is needed:

1. *The lowermost eye on each cane must be suffered to
grow at will without being checked or interfered with.*

2. *The tops of the shoots, pushing from all other eyes,
are pinched two leaves above the uppermost bunch, not
counting the leaf near the bunch.*

These golden rules contain a wisdom which cannot be
valued too highly. The shoot, being pinched, cannot continue growing; consequently there will be an abundance
of sap for the nourishment of the clusters. The two
leaves are needed, and sufficient to make the grapes sweet.
As the upper eyes of the shoot cannot push, the eye of
the lowermost node grows the more vigorously, and makes
a strong cane for the next year. The spurs, may they be
short or long, are likewise intended for strong canes, hence

it follows that one shoot, if possible the lowermost on each cane, must not be pinched, but must grow undisturbed to the end of the year, when it is to be pruned as a cane.

The first pinching of the vine may be performed before it blossoms, as soon as the buds are distinctly visible. The earlier the vine is pinched, the less nourishing substance it loses.

However easy the above rules appear to be, yet their practical application is not quite so easy. There are one or two eyes in the axil of the foot stalk on the green shoot ; *those eyes which are green and soft, ought also to be removed.* This can easily be accomplished with the nail of a finger or the thumb ; for they push, if not removed, and absorb a part of the sap, destined to nourish the bunch, and lessen the vigor of the lowermost eye of the cane which is intended for a cane the next year. It is therefore advisable to perform these two operations simultaneously ; after the top of the shoot has been pinched two leaves above the uppermost bunch, all eyes in the sinuses of the foot stalks of the leaves must be destroyed; only the lowermost shoot must be left to grow at will. Pinching, during the time of blossoming, is not to be recommended, because the blossoms are easily injured.

There exists no other reason for it, although some think it is indispensable not to do anything to the vine during the time of blossoming, as though during that time it were more sensitive to bear external influences than at any other. I have also, during blossoming time, carefully pinched shoots, and have never found any difference from what it would have been, or was, when it was performed before or after that time.

After blossoming, the vine grows more vigorously. The eyes, remaining on the shoots, push and form little shoots, which are called *laterals.*

In the axil of the leaf stalk there are always at least

two eyes, of which alternately the left, the next time the right eye pushes and forms a lateral. If the laterals that have been produced are removed, the other eye soon commences pushing ; if the lateral of the second eye is rubbed off, a third dormant eye is formed, etc. This shows that the laterals perform an important service in regard to the dormant eyes. As long as the lateral is growing, the eye at the base of it remains dormant ; if it is removed, it receives an abundance of sap and pushes. *This is the reason why no laterals on the shoot intended for a cane, that is, on the lowermost shoot, should be rubbed off.*

Although soon after the removal of the shoot a new eye is formed, yet this takes place later and later, and the eye does not last so long as that which has pushed in the spring, and, therefore, in the course of the summer, is not fully developed for producing a blossom. It is one of the commonest mistakes made by vintners to remove these laterals without any discrimination, because they consider them to be robbers of strength. The laterals of the shoot to be preserved for a cane are destined to receive the sap and preserve the eye, growing at its base in its dormant state.

The laterals continue pushing from the canes during the whole summer ; it is, therefore, necessary to have a certain and infallible criterion, in going over a vine, to know which laterals must be removed, and which must remain. This is contained in the following rule :

3. *It is useful to remove the laterals of the shoots that have been pinched ; they must remain on the shoot not pinched, i. e., on the lowermost.*

The remaining leaves of a vine, regularly pinched, grow large and very solid in a short time, and the lowest shoots not pinched grow with great vigor. The pinched shoots soon attain the size, beyond which they cannot increase in length, as they cannot grow at the top, and the laterals are removed as soon as they appear. The shoots, on the con-

trary, not pinched or interfered with, because intended for
bearing the next spring, grow in the course of the summer from eight to ten, and sometimes even twenty feet
long. This does not create any difficulty when the vines
are grown on trellises, because there is room enough to
arrange and tie them. If the strips of the trellis are in a
vertical position, projecting above, those shoots are carried
behind them, where they are permitted to grow. If the
trellises are made of horizontal wires, the shoots in question are tied to the uppermost, on which they are suffered
to grow in a horizontal position. In vineyards where
posts are used, the shoots are tied to them as far as their
length goes; the upper ends of the shoots swing either in
the air or they are tied to the post of the next vine. I
anticipate that I shall get in conflict with many practical
vignerons who are in the habit of cutting off the shoots
in August as far as they think proper, to re-establish order
and to obviate and further confusion. This practice, however, is altogether erroneous, because, after the shoots intended for canes have been shortened, the dormant eyes
commence pushing; so a part of the eyes destined to bear
the next year is lost, and the crop is lessened. Those laterals, although developed so late, grow so large that they
must be pinched again. A shoot not pinched is sometimes difficult to manage on account of its length, but
those pinched, much more so, on account of the number of
their laterals. If the principle is correct that the shoots
intended for canes must not be injured, it is necessary to
provide means for their support. *A vine may be grown
as large or as small as it is convenient; yet the length
of the shoots destined to bear next year cannot be arbi-
trarily reduced to a certain measure.*

Even in the smallest vine they will be from six to eighteen feet long, and they must, at all events, be provided for
without shortening them. When I was riding, in the fall
of 1862, through the Rheingau, I saw the vines kept

neatly about four feet high; the shoots, however, which were to bear next year, had produced many laterals. The yellowish-green color of the young shoots shows this; they have not been long enough exposed to the light to be as green as older leaves. These young laterals are especially liable to be attacked by the grape disease. In the second part of the summer, no such yellowish-green shoots must be found on the vine. It is true that they continue pushing from the pinched shoots, but they must be rubbed off as soon as they appear; they do not push from the shoots intended for bearing next year, if the error of shortening them is avoided. Where, in the second part of the summer, yellowish-green shoots appear on a vine, regularly pinched, then they may be removed unhesitatingly. The confusion of a vine, treated in the right manner, will never be so great as many believe; for the bearing canes are pinched and remain small, and there are but a few long shoots destined for bearing the next year; their number is not much greater than that of the canes which bear fruit. It is judicious to grow a few more shoots than are to be retained for canes; this has the advantage that the best may be selected in the fall, and that those that are weaker may be removed by pruning, in order to restore the proper number. The shade from these long shoots is of no account, because the rays of the sun, falling upon the leaves of the long shoot, have the same effect as if they had struck the vine itself. It is necessary that the long shoot should vegetate and develop in the light of the sun, so that the cane itself, of course, must produce shade. If a part of a vine is in the shade from a shoot growing on a vine before it, the shoots of that vine are exposed to the full rays of the sun, and it receives from above the light intercepted from below by the vine before it. In planting grape vines on a plain, or on a gentle declivity, shade cannot be avoided; if one part of a vine is entitled to the sun, the other must be contented to be, for a certain time, in

the shade. Moreover, only the leaf of the vine ought to
be exposed to the full light of the sun, while the cluster
is to develop and to ripen in the diffused light of day.

GRAPE VINE PLANTATIONS.

There is hardly any other plant so well adapted to varia-
tion of management as the grape vine. It is not our
purpose to give here detailed directions concerning the arrangements of plantations, but only hints which may
be useful, where a skillful gardener can be consulted.
There exists no system of cultivating the vine which could
be called absolutely the best for all regions; the climate,
as well as the nature of the variety of the vine, requires
particular attention.

All methods are successful to a certain degree, and there
is none not considered the best by some. So much is true—
that, of all plants, the vine gives the most ample reward
for the care bestowed upon it, and that many a vacant
spot of a garden may be used for planting a choice variety,
so that it may be turned to account.

VINES TRAINED ALONG THE GARDEN WALK.

By this, low, horizontal branches of grape vines are
meant, growing at considerable distances from each other,
the canes and foliage of which do not occupy any useful
space. They are trained above edgings of box and
strawberries without interfering with their growth. For
this arrangement, such walks in the garden are selected as
are parallel to the longest extent of it. The whole length
is divided into equal parts of five or six feet each, and
those places are marked by small sticks. Supposing the
distance of six feet is preferred, a hole is dug at the first
stick, or six feet from the end, then at the third, fifth,
seventh, etc., skipping the equal numbers' two, four, six,
etc. If each vine sends out on the two opposite sides a

cane of six feet each, the whole length will be covered by
the vine, and, therefore, the two last vines are planted six
feet from the end or beginning. A vine is now planted,
either a cutting or a root, in each hole, in a straight line
along the margin of the walk; the roots must be so arranged and so disposed, that they must grow into the beds
where they find better soil and can be manured. They
are protected by sticks against injury from footsteps, and
are watered during the summer, if necessary. In the fall,
each young vine is cut down to two eyes, from which
two shoots are suffered to grow the next year. As they
do not bear, they may be laid on the ground behind the
edgings. In the third year, a strong iron wire, at least
one-twelfth of an inch in diameter, is stretched between
the first and the last post; the wire is supported by a thin
post near each vine. The wire ought to be stretched at
the height of eighteen or twenty inches above the ground.
In this way, the bed remains open to the view, and the edging plants, growing under the canes, are not injured, as they
receive sufficient light. The two posts at the extreme ends
ought to be made of oak wood three inches square; their
ends ought to be also square, not round. If they are three
and a half feet long, each two feet will be *in*, and a foot and
a half above the ground. They are strong enough to bear
the stress of the wire. Near the upper end each of the
two posts receives towards the middle a strong iron hook,
with a screw cut at its end; it is screwed into the post, so
that the opening of the hook is on the upper side. A hole
of a quarter of an inch in diameter is bored through the
other post, through which a strong piece of iron wire is
put, being bent in the form of a hook on the inside, and
having a screw with a four-cornered nut on the outside.
The small posts, set to each vine along the whole side of
the walk, are also of oak, and if they are a foot and a half
deep in the soil, they will have strength enough. In order
to stretch the wire, an eye is made on one of its ends,

through which the hook passes; it is then hooked into the wire of the second end post, which terminates in a screw, so that it touches the tops of the intermediate small posts. Then it is stretched by means of the screw and nut as much as possible. The wire is kept in position on the tops of the intermediate posts by small staples or rings with wood screws. If the stress or the heat lengthens the wire, it is stretched again by turning the nut of the screw. Even without such an apparatus, the wire may be stretched by wooden wedges and stones driven into the soil by the posts, in order to straighten them. As the wire is shortened by the cold of the winter, it is advisable to loosen it a little, and to stretch it again when the vines are tied up in the next spring.

Others recommend to use strips of wood instead of wire; they must be nailed on the tops of the posts. Strips are less durable and more expensive than wires; for the place where they are nailed is apt to rot, owing to the oxide of iron produced by the rusting nail; and if the strip breaks there, and is an inch too short, it must be replaced by a new one. Wires have little body, and the tying to a wire is easier than to a thick, clumsy strip. The durability of the wires is increased by giving them a coat of oil paint. The color is given by mixing it with pure red lead. This color shows the place of the wire, and prevents occasional visitors from injuring themselves in stepping over a place not yet filled with canes of the vine. The canes, growing in the second year, are tied in the third, right and left to the wire, and are suffered to bear. It is necessary to pinch and remove shoots, if this method of training is adopted. One of the lowest shoots on each side must not be pinched or interfered with, as it is to be used as a cane for bearing the next year; all other bearing shoots, when pinched just beyond the second leaf above the last cluster, cannot grow longer. The shoots for canes are tied to the same wire, but below it, which compels them to lengthen in a straight line.

The canes which have borne fruit are cut off in the next autumn ; the new canes are pruned to twelve or fourteen buds, and also some spurs are provided for, so that it is possible, after the lapse of some years, to shorten the stem and to go back again, nearer to the first starting point. It is very easy always to have two strong canes covering, with the exception of the extremities, the intervals of twelve feet of the wire, except at the end. That space is needed for tying the shoots of the uppermost buds. If a post, seven feet high, is set to each vine, two additional fruiting canes, as well as the shoots for canes, may be tied to it ; so the crop may be very much increased.

On such a cordon, eight hundred feet long, I have grown, in the fourth year after planting, so many bunches, that I made from them one-half awme (30 gallons) of excellent, red wine, without using a single square foot of the surface of the garden for it.

Only here and there some plants of the box, which formed the edging, were taken out to make room for the vines. The rays of the sun, intercepted by the vines, would have fallen during one-half of the day upon the walks, during the other upon the box and other worthless plants, which attained, however, their perfect development. The variety was of the early Burgundy variety.

TRELLISES ON WALLS.

A wall, exposed to the sun during one-half of the day, towards the east, south or west, or intermediate between them, may be used for a trellis. A southern or south-westerly is the best ; early ripening sorts succeed also when exposed to the east or west, provided the climate is not unfavorable.

The walls for trellises are generally whitewashed, because it is cheapest. Yet it is better to add something to it that makes the wash darker, to absorb more heat. For this purpose, any brown coloring matter, mixed with white-wash, will answer to make a dark-colored wall. Without the mixture of whitewash, the pulverized coloring matter is washed off by the rain from the walls. *Umber and lampblack may be used, yet Manganese is much to be preferred.

A wall, covered with blue slate, absorbs the greatest amount of heat ; the cheapest kind of slate or refuse of slate answers a very good purpose. Blue slate, exposed to the full sun, is heated to fifty to fifty-five degrees Reaum. (to 145 or 156° Fahr.) The wall, not shaded by the foliage, is heated by the rays of the sun, and imparts warmth to the currents of rising air, which give off their warmth to the vine.

A great amount of heat is accumulated in the wall from the sun, the effect of which is felt even at night. In passing by a wall, shone upon by the sun during the day, after sunset the undulations of the warmth are distinctly felt in the face. This advantage of being heated for a longer time can be given to the vines by painting the wall dark. Wire trellises are now preferred to wooden ones, not only on account of their durability, but also on account of their greater cheapness. They can, besides, be erected and arranged in a very short time. The wire must be at least one-twelfth of an inch thick, and annealed, so that it may be bent without breaking. It is best to stretch the wire in a horizontal direction. In this case, there are not many places where the vine is to be tied, nor can a vine which has been tied, slide down. A trellis five or six feet high requires but three or four wires, the lowest, a foot from the ground, the others, in distances of sixteen inches from each other. Strong pieces of iron are fastened to the extreme ends of the wall, in order to stretch the wire ; every twelve feet, the wire must be passed through a thinner piece of iron, in order to keep it in place. It is necessary to mark first the places at the extreme ends with a cross, the middle of which, where the two lines intercept each other, indicates the place where the iron has to be fixed. As such a trellis lasts a long time, it is advisable to measure the distance with a rule, carefully. After the strong pieces of iron at the two ends of the wall have been fastened, the whole length is divided into equal parts of ten or twelve feet each, and there a perpendicular line is made with a piece of charcoal or. a carpenter's lead pencil. Then a piece of cord or twine is stretched between the two strong irons, which crosses the black lines at right angles; the places where the cord crosses the black lines are to be marked red. Here the thinner irons are fastened, which are to serve to keep the wire in place. To drive a pointed iron in mortar or brick walls is easy enough, but stone walls cause a great deal more trouble. Frequently it is necessary to try to the right and left, till a place is found where two stones are put together; for it is impossible to penetrate into the stones themselves. In order not to spoil many points of the pieces of soft iron, a four-cornered punch of steel, which has been tempered blue, and has a handle, is used. Should the hole become too large by this operation, a piece of pine wood is driven into it with a hammer, and then the iron is driven into the pine wood. It is left to the judgment of the person who makes the trellis, whether he will make use of an apparatus to stretch the wires by means of screws and nuts. The wires receive a coat of red paint; they last, so painted, much longer, and are always visible.

A wire trellis well arranged and firm will likely last longer than the life of him who has made it.

FREE TRELLISES.

It is much more profitable and advantageous to erect grape trellises on gentle declivities than to plant single vines. The number of posts required is much less, and the greater extent of the root in vines growing strong will involve less expense, and give a greater produce. A vine trained on a trellis ten or twelve feet wide, and four or four and a half feet high, bears as many clusters as eight or ten vineyard vines trained to posts. Also the labor of pruning, tying and manuring is much simpler and easier than in a larger number of single vines.

As regards the direction of the trellises, practical men differ. Kecht advises the direction from north to south, that is, parallel to the meridian. This arrangement has the disadvantage that in the hottest part of the day, the sun shines into the spaces between the rows, heating the ground, while the rows are in their own shade. It is, however, much more important that the *vine* should be warmed than the *ground*. I have, therefore, chosen just the opposite direction, that is, from east to west, in a plantation of vines. As the line of the rows is a little inclined towards the meridian, it so happens that the sun at one o'clock, p. m., shines vertically upon the rows. Consequently my plantation enjoys the sun in the following manner: Before seven o'clock, a. m., the sun shines on the back part of the trellises; at seven o'clock it shines between the rows from east; from seven o'clock, a. m., till seven o'clock, p. m., the front part of the trellis enjoys the sunshine; at seven o'clock, p. m., the rays of the sun strike the spaces between the rows, and after seven o'clock the back part of the trellises again.

In the hottest part of the day, from ten o'clock, a. m., till three o'clock, p. m., the sun is almost vertical above the rows, and they are then in the condition of trellises made on walls with a southern exposure, which exposure has always been preferred to all others. In the hottest part of the day, the ground is shaded so that it does not dry so rapidly. My aim was to intercept all the rays of the sun, that would fall upon that piece of ground, by the plant itself, as this would insure the best success. It is true that I have no experience yet, but the arrangement was planned with so much care, that I am confident of a favorable result. A little deviation from this direction may be desirable if the natural condition of the situation of the ground is different. Should it be so situated as to receive the shadow from a near mountain in the afternoon, it will be advantageous to turn the whole arrangement a little eastward, and plant the rows so that the sun shines into them in the morning and in the evening at five o'clock; it will then, at eleven a. m., be vertically above them.

If the ground lies open in all directions, it is better to deviate a little towards the west, because the afternoon is always hotter than the forenoon. If the shadow of a mountain falls from the east upon the plantation, it may be so arranged that it has the sun vertical at two o'clock, p. m., but always so that the sun does not shine into the spaces between the rows during the hottest time of the day.

If the direction is ascertained, the east and west sides of the ground are to be divided into equal parts, each four feet wide; this is the distance of the trellises from each other. Then the north and south sides of the piece must be divided into parts of ten feet each.

Each vine is to cover five feet of trellis on each side, consequently ten feet in the whole. No vines must, therefore, be planted at the east and west terminus of the rows, but five feet from it. The last post, however, is to be planted at the terminus itself. Now the holes are dug in the places indicated, and the plants or cuttings are so placed that they are in straight lines; this may easily be accomplished by another person sighting at the last hole, marked by some prominent object, along a straight pole, placed horizontally. In the first year, the green shoots may lie and grow on the ground; in the second, they may be tied to sticks, and the spaces between the rows *may* be used for cultivating vegetables. In the third year, the trellis must be erected. For this purpose strong posts, three inches square, the points of which are four cornered, are driven into the ground at the east and west side of the rows; if they are two and a half feet in the ground, and five feet above it, they are long enough. Between them, thinner posts two inches square, but equally high as the larger ones, are driven into the ground near every vine, i. e., in distances of ten feet from each other to support the wires ; the two last rows east and west may, of course, be skipped. Instead of oaken posts, which are expensive, round, pine saplings may be used, but they must be impregnated with sulphate of copper. This can be done by dissolving ten or twelve pounds of sulphate of copper in an old hogshead, by pouring hot water on it, stirring it frequently. Ten or twelve posts are put in it, and remain five or six days, when they are to be replaced by others, while the first set is dried. So much water is to be added that the hogshead with the posts in it is full. As long as sulphate of copper remains undissolved at the bottom, the absorbed or evaporated water must be replenished. Of all the materials used for impregnating wood to make it durable, (kyanizing,) sulphate of copper is one of the cheapest and most effective.

To give a good coat of coal tar to the part impregnated, after the posts are dry, will protect them still more effectually.

To stretch the wire, strong conical pieces of iron may be used, similar to those used for stretching piano strings. They must be made to fit holes bored with a tapering bit, flattened at the top, and pierced with a hole. The iron must be driven into the hole, so that it bears the stress by friction alone. The force applied in stretching is so great that the posts may yield and turn a little. To prevent

this, the lowest wire is fastened to the front part (south
side) of the post, the second to the back side

The lowest wire is to be stretched about a foot from the
ground; the others at distances from twelve to sixteen
inches. Four wires will make a trellis five feet high.

We will now compare such an arrangement with a vineyard of single vines trained to poles. Supposing the piece
of ground is eighty feet square, there will be twenty-one
trellises, if the rows are four feet distant from each other.
As each vine covers ten feet of the trellis, there will be
eight vines in a row, consequently 168 in the whole. If a
vineyard is planted of single vines three and a half feet
apart each way, there will be 24 vines in a row, that is,
576 vines in the whole. But if the vines are planted three
feet apart each way, as it is usually done, there will be
729 vines and posts. Although it is impossible to estimate
the first cost of each of these arrangements, even approx-
imately, as the prices of the posts, as well as those of the
wire, vary very much; yet trellised vines cover the whole
space, and consequently bear much more abundantly than
vines trained to posts, so that trellises are proper and more
profitable than posts.

VINES TRAINED TO TRELLISES.

The bearing canes of vines, occupying a trellis ten or
twelve feet wide, or five or six feet high, may be grown in
the middle, and evenly destributed over it, in the shape of
a fan. From eight to ten canes are sufficient, and they
may be easily grown on a stem only a few feet in extent.
Figure 5 represents such a vine, immediately after pruning
in the fall. The canes which have borne have been already removed, but the places of the cuts of the shoots,
intended for canes, are only indicated. Also some spurs
are to be seen at A and B; the shoots which will start from

their buds will enable the vine dresser to reduce the height of the stem in the following year. If only two branches

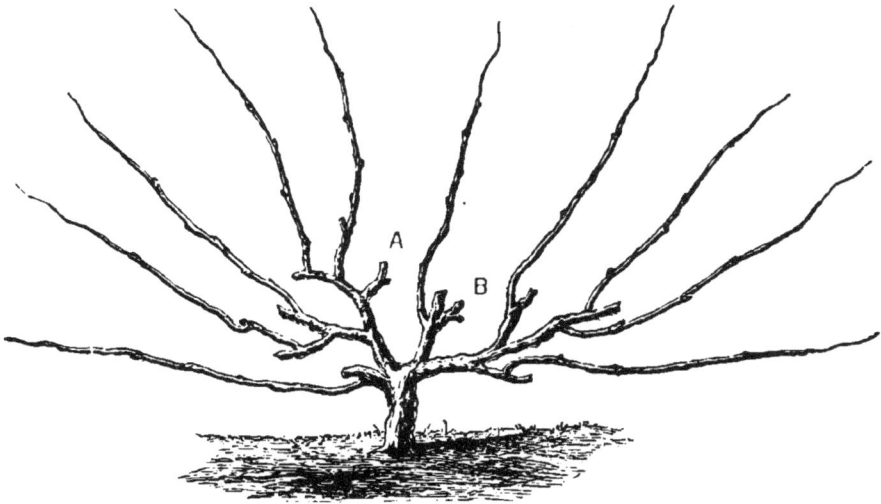

Fig. 5.—VINE ON TRELLIS, PRUNED.

of the stem are shortened every year, the vine will always be kept within moderate bounds.

J. P. BRONNER'S METHOD.

According to this method all branches and shoots form right angles with the stems and canes from which they grow. [Whether Bronner had any knowledge of Speechly's and Hoare's plan I cannot tell, although it is hardly probable.—*Translator.*] It is very similar to the methods adopted at Thomery and Fontainebleau, where nearly all the grapes are grown which are consumed at Paris. It is the special object of this method to cause an equal distribution of the sap, and to cover the whole trellis equally with bearing canes. It is adapted to free trellises, as well as to such as are arranged on walls. The form of the right angle is especially adapted to walls with windows and doors, as it is in conformity with them. The dis-

3

tances between the vines, trained to a free trellis, may be eight or ten feet; for those on walls, twelve feet and more.

All strips and wires must run in a horizontal direction; the unequal numbers, three, five, seven, etc., according to the height, must be preserved. The first wire must be stretched a foot from the ground; the others at distances of sixteen inches each.

A single trellis consists of three wires; the two arms are tied to the lowest, and the bearing canes are tied in a vertical direction to the two next wires. A double trellis consists of five wires, and has horizontal arms tied to the first and third; the canes from the third wire are to be tied to the fourth and fifth.

A trellis of three stories consists of seven wires, having arms on the first, third and fifth; the canes of the fifth are to be tied to the sixth and seventh. We will now consider the management of a single trellis with three wires. Before the vine can be trained to it, it must have attained vigor and a good size.

A vine, two years old, when planted in the fall, must be cut down to one eye. The shoot, pushing from it, must not be interfered with; it must grow undisturbed without pinching and stopping. This treatment will tend to produce fibrous roots.

In the following year, the vine is to be cut down to two buds, and should, in the next year, the two canes not be

Fig. 6.—FIRST PRUNING.

so thick as a child's finger, they must be cut down again, and treated as described. If a cutting is planted, it will require at least three years to make it strong enough for training. The third year of the growth of the young vine is, therefore, the first of the training. The two years' plant, having grown a year in the place assigned to it, makes in the summer a shoot to be pruned to two eyes in the fall. Figure 6.

These two buds will produce two shoots in the following (the second) year, figure 7, which are left four feet long at pruning, and are changed to brown canes in the fall. There will be a great many buds on them, which

Fig. 7.—SECOND PRUNING.

will all push in the next spring. Four are selected on each arm, on the upper side of it, and distributed as equally as possible, (figure 8); the green shoots proceeding from them must be suffered to grow undisturbed, while all the other buds must be rubbed off. In this way, eight shoots will be obtained at nearly equal distances from each other, which are to be tied vertically to the two upper wires as

Fig. 8.—PRUNING THE CANES.

soon as they reach them. In the (third) fall the unequal numbers *one* and *three* of the shoots, being now canes, are pruned back to two buds, but the equal numbers *two* and *four* to three buds. Figure 8.

In the following (the fourth) year one shoot of the spurs, corresponding to the unequal numbers, and pruned to two eyes, is suffered to grow, but the other is rubbed off, because it was only left on account of the possibility of an accident to either of them. The shoots, pruned to the three buds, (the equal numbers,) will bear fruit; they must be pinched, as explained, and no green shoot must

Fig. 9.—FIRST YEAR OF FRUITING.

be permitted to grow. The lowest buds of a cane being mostly wood buds, only the third buds will show blossoms. Figure 9.

This will not weaken the vine. In the fall of the fourth year, the canes of the unequal numbers are pruned to five or six eyes, as shown in figure 9, but the equal numbers, having borne fruit, to two eyes.

In the following (the fifth) year, the canes of the unequal numbers will bear along their whole length for the first time, figure 10, and each of the spurs of the equal numbers will produce a strong shoot for a bearing cane. Now everything remains in the same order, the equal and unequal numbers alternately bearing or making shoots. As the shoot on the strong arm retains but one bud in the year in which this is to be grown for a cane, it receives an abundance of sap to make the canes strong ; and as the bearing canes on the same arms are not permitted to make a single shoot, they are supplied with ample nourishment for perfecting fruit. The functions of all the parts of the vine are performed alternately, so that none of them is taxed too heavily.

If a double trellis is to be covered, more time is required; the upper story must not be made to bear in the same year as the lower, but several years later, and so on.

Each branch growing from an arm must be regarded as an independent vine, as it were, which is prolonged every

Fig. 10.—SECOND YEAR OF FRUITING.

year by a joint. The same means which are employed to reduce the height of a vine, must be used in managing a branch. The shoots pushing from wood eyes on the old wood must be suffered to grow; they are pruned in the fall to spurs from which a shoot is grown to replace the old wood above it.

It is frequently necessary to train a vine so that the bearing canes are at considerable distance from the ground, for instance, in streets and yards where people are going to and fro. . A cane, tied in a vertical direction to the wall, must then be grown as a stem, without any branches whatever: Only the leaves are left, as long as it is an object to strengthen it. If the uppermost bud is permitted to push, the height is soon reached where the horizontal arms are desired, which have to rest on wires. It is important not to reach the height too soon. If four feet are added annually to the height of the stem, the arms and bearing canes will be so high that they cannot be touched by a person on the ground. The arrangement just described, according to which bearing canes and shoots are grown alternately along the horizontal wires, is very well adapted

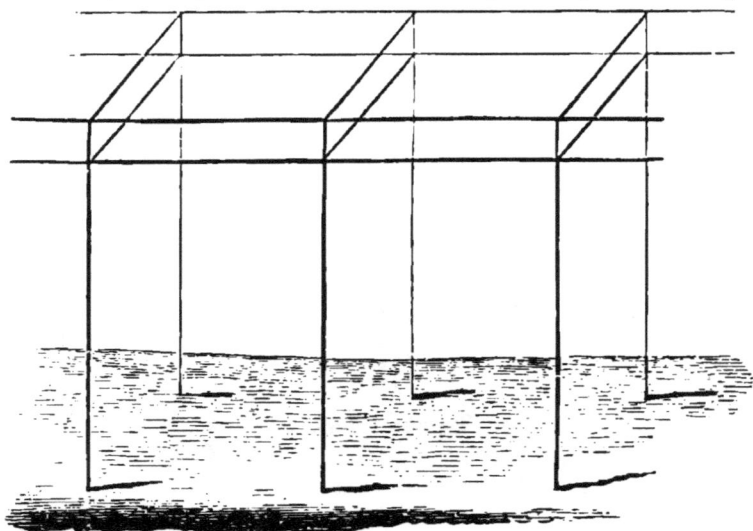

Fig. 11.—ARCADE TRELLIS.

for this purpose. The height of the space between two windows of a house affords room enough for a second wire to tie the bearing canes to it. Vines may be planted in a great many other places to make them profitable, and to embellish them, as near the columns of a verandah, to cover the wire roof of a poultry yard, etc. If the principles of the management are understood, their application to a given case is not difficult. Arbors, covered with grape vines, ought, under no circumstances, to be clothed with vines on both sides and above, because it will make the inside moist and shady, so that the grapes will not ripen perfectly. An excellent arrangement for growing table grapes is the so-called *arcade arbor*, of which only the outlines can be given here. The framework, made of wood, is indicated, figure 14, by straight lines.

Strong posts are set at equal distances from each other, of seven or eight feet, on which two trellis strips or wires, a foot and a half or two feet distant, are arranged. A vine is planted to each post, trained up to the first strip, and two arms from it are laid in along the strip.

A height of seven or eight feet from the ground to the lowest strip is sufficient, according as it may be desirable to have the clusters higher or lower. Roses may be grown between the vines, especially if the stem has no branches. Such an arcade is, as it were, a vineyard in the air, which makes little shade, so that the beds below may be used for growing anything on them; it is beautiful to look at, and yields large crops.

TIME REQUIRED FOR COVERING A TRELLIS.

This is the place to discuss the question how soon the space of a certain trellis may be covered. If the canes are pruned long, that is, to sixteen or twenty buds, a vine may be made to cover a large space in a few years, but so rapid a process has disadvantages peculiar to itself. The extension of the vine ought always to correspond to the probable development of the roots. As they are in the ground, not exposed to view, judgment must be exercised by taking into consideration the length of the time, the fertility of the soil, and the vigor, the length, and the number of the growing shoots. If the process is hastened, and numerous shoots are left in the third and fourth years, the root cannot furnish as much nourishment as is needed. Many shoots push, show blossoms, and remain feeble, and in spite of regular pinching, the lowest eyes do not push vigorously. They yield many bunches of small size; they will not be sweet, and will ripen late. In the next fall the canes are changes to stems ; there are no strong shoots to make good canes in the fall. The shoots grow very high on the stem, which has grown to an enormous extent.

This results from pruning a vine too long. In this case it is necessary to prune down to the old wood, in order to produce few, but more vigorous shoots. The crop, after a rich harvest, will be small; the advantage, gained by the prematurely hastened production, will be lost, and the development of the vine will be put back a year. If this circumstance is always kept in view, the temptation to obtain an abundant crop by long pruning will be easily resisted.

It is only the question whether the covering by a vine of a space twelve feet wide shall be accomplished two or three years sooner. A slower procedure is much preferable, as it makes both the stems and the roots stronger. *How long a vine ought to be pruned, that is, how many eyes ought to be left, is different in different kinds of grapes. The cluster never grows from the first bud of the shoot, and not lower than from the fourth and fifth; likewise the lowest buds of the canes rarely bear fruit. There are kinds which bear fruit on shoots from the seventh and eight bud ; there are others, like the Chasselas, which bear grapes on the lowest shoots.*

Should the former be pruned below the seventh eye, then all the fruit bearing buds would be cut off, and only wood buds would be left; consequently they would not bear fruit. This explains the experience of all vinyardists that close pruning produces much wood and little fruit, because the eyes, organized for blooming, are cut off. The opinion is pretty generally prevalent that if the supply of sap should be too abundant, only wood and no fruit would be produced, and that the fruit only requires a very moderate supply of sap. This opinion is, no doubt, erroneous, as the fruit demands more nourishment than any other part of the plant. This is sufficiently proven by the fact that an abundant crop prevents the vigorous development of the branches very much.

The same takes place in regard to apples and pears. Too close pruning produces only wood shoots, not, however, on account of a super-abundance of sap, but because the fruit buds, which grow more towards the end of the shoots, have been cut off. On the other hand we find that our rule holds good, namely, that we have to prune very close, in order to obtain strong wood for the next year, even if the rich crops of the current year should be lost. It would be foolish to grow, as unskilled gardeners do, every year nothing but wood and very little fruit. *A general knowledge of the varieties, in regard to the eyes, which will be fruitful, is a sure guide. Varieties bearing higher up must be pruned to twelve or fifteen buds ; the lower bearing ones to six or eight eyes.* To the former belong the varieties from the South, such as Malvasier and the like, often, also, kinds ripening late ; those that ripen early, and are accustomed to our climate, as the *Chasselas,* bear on the lower eyes.

MANURING.

The grape vine, like all other plants, takes from the soil certain constituents which must be replaced to grow them successfully. They are the so-called mineral ingredients which cannot be supplied by the atmosphere. To them belong especially potash and phosphoric acid, combined with lime.

If the culture of the vine could be so managed that only the alcohol and the sugar were taken from the vineyard, and that all other things taken from the vine were given back to the soil of the vineyard, no other manuring would be needed. But along with the wine, also tartar, and in this the potash is sold, as well as phosphate of lime. All the tartar sold and bought is derived from wine,

3*

and contains potash, of which the soil of the vineyard has been robbed. If that is not restored, and if it does not exist in the soil in the greatest abundance, the growth of the vine must be impaired. It is a fact that in former years the vine was planted in plains to a much greater extent than at present; so, many places in the Margraviate Brandenburg designate some tracts of land by calling them vineyards, though not a single vine is now growing there. An animal cannot form bones except by such food as contains phosphate of lime; a hen cannot lay eggs with hard shells, if her nourishment does not contain lime. The vine cannot form tartar when it is wanting in potash, and the tartar, as it appears, is formed like the bones and the shell of the eggs, because it is never wanting, and the plant ceases growing without a full supply of potash. For these reasons, the culture of the vine has ceased in regions with little potash in the soil, after it had languished for a number of years without giving any profit. In plains it is impossible to restore the potash, except by man itself; but who could be induced to supply it without knowing the cause of the failure? In mountainous districts the cause is very different; the soil near the Moselle, the Rhine, the Nahe, and the Ahr consists of argillaceous slate; there the stones are spread all over the inclined plains of the vineyards, so that not a single square inch of the soil remains uncovered, and the vineyards look more like quarries than plantations of vines. During the whole winter the stones, containing frequently as much as three per cent. of potash, are disintegrated by the weather, and the little particles are washed down into the soil by rain and melting snow, and supply there the loss caused by the removal of the last crop. As long as stones of this are abundant in those vineyards, potash is not wanting; therefore the softest of such stones are preferred; and where they are not found in small pieces, they are severed from the rocks with sledge hammers, and even with powder, to cover the clean soil of the vineyards with them, although this requires much labor.

This is manuring with minerals in the best form, although it is the general belief that the stones serve only for warming the soil, and for preventing it from being carried off by heavy rains. They are effective in this respect also, it is true, but they yield potash, and supply that which has been abstracted. It is the chief benefit derived from them.

Should any one be skeptical, he can easily convince himself by taking for this purpose stones, destitute of potash. The experience of a few years will be sufficient to show him the value of stones, containing potash. In Deidesheim, on the Haardt Mountains, disintegrated basalt is carried into the vineyards at great expense. There the soil in the plains contains but little potash, not enough to supply the vines in adequate proportions. Experience has taught people that stones carried into the vineyards from so great a distance yield the supply needed; it is manuring with minerals. Basalt contains from two to four per cent of potash. But not only potash, but also phosphate of lime must be restored, which is generally done by cow manure. It is true, cow manure contains phosphate of lime, and a sufficient quantity of potash. If we had always a sufficient supply of it, the potash, as well as, especially, the phosphate of lime, carried off in the wine, would be restored to the soil. But cow manure is getting daily more expensive, and enough of it cannot be procured. When it shall have reached a certain price, vineyard culture, which does not yield even now in our region a certain crop every year, will not be profitable any more; we have nearly arrived at that point.

The cause why the price of cow manure is rising daily, lies simply in the fact that the potash and phosphate of lime have been abstracted from the fields to such a degree that they are exhausted. If the farmer cannot grow

clover, he has no feed for his cows, and cannot sell manure
The number of farmers whose fields are becoming unproductive is rapidly increasing, so that the price of manure
must rise rapidly, because it is getting very scarce. The
fields of the farmers are impoverished when they sell the
manure, and do not use it for fertilizing their own fields.
It is an incontrovertible fact that the land is impoverished
by selling the products of agriculture, *even without selling
manure ;* how much more certain and rapid will be its
ruin, if, in addition to the products, the manure also is sold.
A farmer who sells manure is a prodigal living on his capital ; he lights his candle simultaneously at both ends.
For a man who cannot resist the temptation to sell his
manure, the day is already appointed on which his field
will come under the hammer, and which will make him
either an emigrant or a beggar.   Emigration is a proof of
the exhaustion of the soil ; thus the culture of vineyards
becomes a curse to an agricultural country.   It hangs like
a vampire on the neck of the country, sucking the potash
and phosphate of lime.   It is my intention to stir up the
farmers not to sell any more (not even an ounce,) manure
to the owners of vineyards, for the interest of both.   If
the land of the farmers is ruined by selling manure, the
owners of vineyards cannot get from them what they need,
so that they will be forced at last to become independent
of them.   It is my ardent wish that this may take place
before the farmer is ruined.

The vinyardist will buy manure as long as it is offered
to him at a suitable price ; he can console himself, should
a farmer be ruined, by buying his field at the sheriff's
sale.   As it is the farmer who is ruined first, he ought
to commence resistance, and to refuse to sell manure, or
to ask such a price that he can buy double the value of
it in bone dust, guano and wood ashes.   He must use the
money received for the manure in buying the materials
just mentioned, and give them back to his fields.

Should the farmer get only sufficient money for his manure to buy an equivalent of bone dust, he has not sold at a profit. If, on the contrary, the vinyardist has to pay double the amount for cow manure that he does for an equivalent in bone dust or leached ashes, he will cease buying manure, and will prefer to buy bone dust for his money, of which he receives double the value as a manure for the same amount. If, however, the vinyardist contends that he cannot do without animal manure, which is not yet proven, he may then pay to the farmer the double price asked ; for error must pay a tax. In this case the vinyardist receives what he wishes, and the farmer has his profit. If the same individual cultivates vineyards as well as fields, he may use his barnyard manure for his vineyards, and bone dust, guano, and leached ashes for his fields. It he cultivates only vineyards, he must become independent of the farmer, who will continue raising the price for manure, so that the vinyardist cannot buy it any more. As soon as the price for manure rises higher than that for an equal quantity of fertilizing material in bone dust and guano, the vinyardist is forced to use them for fertilizing purposes. If a vineyard is situated in a region of argillaceous slate, and if the surface of it is covered with a stratum of this material, only bone dust is required for manuring ; but if the vineyard is in a plain where disintegrated rock cannot be supplied, something besides must be used containing potash, for instance : wood ashes, leached ashes, dust from such roads and turnpikes as are covered with granite, syenite, basalt, and similar rocks containing small proportions of potash ; also soap-suds, chloride of potassium and sulphate of potash. It depends altogether on the price whether the one or the other of the materials mentioned deserves the preference. Of these manuring materials, leached ashes and road dust may be used immediately ; those, however, which are soluble, for instance, wood ashes, soapsuds, chloride of potasssium and

sulphate of potash, require some preparation. All mineral
stuffs, fit for the nourishment of plants, become insoluble
in contact with the soil; to prevent them from reaching
the roots of the vines in a soluble form, they must be
mixed with large quantities of good soil. Sufficient water
is then poured on it to wet it thoroughly, and so it remains long enough for the chemical changes. The result
is an insoluble compound of the soil and the salts of potash, which may be used as manure.

In the fall, some of the soil on the northern side of the
rows is removed, and some of the above compound is laid
there; rain and snow will wash the fertilizing material
into the soil.

It is true, this chemical combination is nearly insoluble
in pure water, but the soil surrounding the roots of the
vine has an affinity for these stuffs, and in virtue of
it, the particles of the salts of potash continue spreading
from grain to grain of the soil until they are evenly distributed. This process is similar to the cementation of
iron, in which the molecules of carbon change their
places without ever having been volatile or liquid.

The carbon gradually penetrates the white-hot, soft iron
bars, until they are changed into steel. Precisely in the
same way mineral substances penetrate in the exhausted soil
from above downwards, and reach the roots in such a condition that they can be absorbed by them without injury.

The roots of the vine are very sensitive to soluble fertilizing materials. Liquid barn-yard manure, incautiously
used, may kill or make them sick. In the summer following
the application of it, the leaves turn yellow, the shoots
that push are feeble, and the fruit remains poor, and does
not mature. Liquid barn-yard manure ought, therefore,
never be brought in direct contact with the roots.

Urine, not decomposed, contains urea, and not yet carbonate of ammonia, and the urine of man, besides, has a large
proportion of common salt. If this liquid manure is to

be used for manuring purposes, it must be prepared in the same way. It must be mixed with sufficient soil to form a stiff paste, which is to be exposed to sunshine and rain. The heat decomposes the urea; it is changed to carbonate of ammonia, and fixed and retained by the soil, while the undecomposed urea filtrates through the soil, and is carried down to the roots. The common salt is not fixed by the soil, and is washed out and carried off by the rain. Liquid manure, so prepared, may, in a solid form, be unhesitatingly used as manure. The method just described, is nearly identical with that of the Japanese, and which that nation, during thousands of years, has followed in the management and preparation of manure, and which has reached us only by a very long and circuitous route. Our barn cellars, built at great expense, and rewarded by premiums as models, are, with exception of the water-tight floor, nothing but humbugs. They have been resorted to through the error of the nitrogenous theory. We attempt to retain in force, what, in contact with the soil, remains of itself, viz.: the ammonia; we guard against sunshine and heat, and prevent thereby the decomposition of the urea; we keep what ought to be washed out, the common salt. But to return to the Japanese method of preparing and managing manure. We.must collect and preserve all the offal obtained from our domestic life to be composted with soil, refuse of straw, etc., and to be exposed to sunshine and rain. Nothing useful is washed out; that which is important and needed undergoes the necessary changes, and that which is injurious is removed. There is, however, another reason why liquid manure ought to be subjected to the process of decomposition and condensation. It is asserted that the disagreeable odor of liquid manure exerts an injurious influence on the perfume of the wine. I have not had any experience of this alleged fact; but I know from experience that liquid manure makes vines sickly.

In Mulder's work, The Chemistry of the Wine, there is
the following passage, (p. 13, of the German translation
by Charles Arenz, Leipsic, 1856) : " It is remarkable that
fetid manure, fecal matter, and the mud of large cities
have an injurious influence upon the perfume of the wine,
while, on the contrary, inodorous manures, which decompose slowly, for instance, wool, horn and bone-black, have
a beneficial effect upon the perfume. The fetid organic
ingredients of the manure pass, therefore, over into the
plants in such a quantity that they are perceivable in the
fruit ; so is the fetid odor of decaying fishes easily distinguished in the cauliflower when manured with them. It
is not without danger to pronounce these facts aloud in a
time in which it is said of the plants that they do not take
up the slightest particle from the soil ; I risk it, however,
to mention the facts."

This passage of Mulder has reference to the principles
of agricultural chemistry established by Liebig to which
Mulder is scientifically, and also personally, opposed, which
is to be regretted. But Mulder could not have found a
better proof for Liebig's principles than just that one before us, which he uses as a weapon against them. If the
odorous ingredients of the manure are such as are perceivable in the plant, they have not been received and assimi-
lated by the plant. Liebig speaks only of the assimilation
of certain bodies by the plant itself. The sugar, the albumen, the fibres in the fetid cauliflower, have assuredly
their origin in inorganic matter ; the organic ingredients
of the decaying fishes in it have not become parts of the
cauliflower. The fact itself proves the necessity of de-
animalizing all manure that is fetid, i. e., to change it as
much as possible to inorganic matter by the aid of atmospheric influences.

In garden and field culture, large heaps of weeds are
accumulating ; they are excellent for receiving liquid manure. They are light and permeable, producing, by the aid

of liquid manure, in a short time a mould, which retains with great tenacity all mineral ingredients. When exposed during the summer, and until January and February, to the influence of sun and rain, and dug over several times, they make a very powerful manure. Offal of the house, of wood stoves, and of bones, is also added. He who cannot obtain cow manure may buy, during the summer, a sufficient supply of horse manure, which can easily be got, because people do not attach much value to it. If managed in the right way, it serves a very good purpose.

It is generally believed that horse manure is too hot. This is a belief not well founded in fact; the assertion is without sense. Horse manure is too light and so much mixed with straw, that it cannot have the same fertilizing power in the same bulk as cow manure. If the horse manure is well prepared and managed during the summer, it can be deprived of its heating power and lightness. It must be composted in alternate layers with garden soil and coal ashes; all bones that have been collected must be put in the horse manure, but not too many in the same place; liquid manure must then be poured over the heap, and this must be covered about four inches deep with garden soil. So prepared, it remains exposed to rain and sun; should a long drouth prevail, it must be sprinkled from the rose of a water-pot. The heaps shrink considerably, but lose not a particle of useful ingredients by evaporation. When dug over from time to time, they make an entirely homogenous and very powerful manure. Frequently this operation is called composting, which, on the whole, does not mean anything definite. It is paramount that the materials used for compost heaps should contain potash and phosphoric acid. Composting exists, then, in such operations as tend to render those mineral materials insoluble in connection with soil, warmth and moisture. Heat offers the conditions of decomposition, and moisture is instrumental in equally distributing and mixing soil and vegetable mould. How often manuring is needed, cannot be determined by a rule that will hold good everywhere and always. If many good years succeed each other, as was the case from 1857 to 1862, five times in six years, a more liberal and frequent application of manure is needed than in the bad years, from 1847 to 1856. This follows directly from the rule: If no fruit is taken from a vineyard, the fertilizing mineral ingredients remain in it; if, on the contrary, the crop is abundant, a very large quantity of potash and phosphoric acid has been taken from the soil. No attention has been paid as yet to this circumstance, so that the application of manure after a bad year was the same as after a good one, as though the mineral manures were removed by the mere lapse of time.

The application of manure ought, without exception, to take place soon after the fall of the leaf, as long as the weather permits it. Some of the soil at the back of the vine, consequently, according to our rule, on the north side, being removed by using the hoe, the manure must be put in the little ditch so made, and must remain uncovered during the whole winter. Rain and snow decompose and carry the manuring materials gradually downward. In the spring, the manure is lightly covered and mixed with the soil, but not so that the roots are injured. Every two, three, or four years, manure is needed. If the weather is favorable, and berries and clusters remain small, while they are abundant and of normal size in neighboring plantations, the soil has not a full supply of mineral matter. If the crop is abundant, it indicates the necessity for manuring, because the mineral matter has been carried off by it. As the vine liberally repays all the care bestowed upon it, there are always causes for better manuring, but not a single one for not giving enough. There is no danger from an overdose of well prepared manure; it will only assist in producing the best possible crops.

On declivities the manure must be placed above the vines in shallow ditches, crossing the vineyard. The soil from them is heaped up on the lower side of them. This soil collects the rain water running down the hill, and keeps it in the ditches filled with manure. It penetrates the soil by a force inherent in it. It is very wrong, as prescribed and taught in many books, to put the manure near the roots. This cannot be effected without injuring them, the mineral manures reaching the roots by cementation and according to the law of gravity. If they are abundant above, they will not be wanting below, in the course of time.

It is in the nature of things that a plant *can be* manured with the offal from it. Rape may be grown on soil manured with oil cake, the refuse of making oil from rape; grape wood, leaves, tendrils, and skins will assist the growth of the vine very much. It is, therefore, very important to take from a vineyard or garden as *little* as possible, and to give back as *much* as possible, or, in other words, nothing but the grape juice must be taken from the vineyard; everything else must be restored to it. The canes cut off in the fall or spring must be chopped into small pieces with a hatchet and mixed with manure. The pressed skins, either before or after distillation, if brandy is made, must be thrown on the compost heap. If all the refuse parts of the vine are used for preparing manure, it reduces the purchase of manure to the smallest figure; it is as impossible to avoid it entirely, as it is impossible to invent a lamp that can be fed with the spare oil. What is sold in the wine itself must be restored to the vineyard from other sources; we lessen it by using the offal from the vine.

If the pressed skins are boiled for distilling alcohol, they are of course nearly valueless for manuring purposes. If, however, Tartaric acid, (which does not cause a loss of the soil,) is made, part of the profit may be used for buying and restoring in a cheaper form the potash taken with

it. The hopes based on manuring vines by using the offal
from them have, therefore, not been realized. Sometimes another way of manuring, with green plants, is
talked of; it is recommended to sow among the vines
vetches, turnips, clover, cereals and the like, and to dig or
plow them under as soon as those plants are fully developed in their growth. This is manuring with the seeds
alone. What those plants have taken from the soil was
already in it, and can therefore not enrich it. Such seeds,
however, are too expensive to use as manure, and the labor
is too great.

All such hopes, founded on imaginary effects of green
manure, have disappeared before the light of exact science.

For a long time an ill-founded importance was ascribed
to digging the soil of the vineyard, and it was recommended to repeat this four or five times during the season.
According to an old proverb, to dig well amounts to slight
manuring, (*Gut gegraben ist halb geduengt,*) and the fa-
ble of the vineyard, in which the sons are said to have
found the hidden treasure in the abundant crops by frequent digging, bears testimony to such a view. It was the
result of the opinion prevailing formerly of the inexhausti-
bility of the soil, in which those who are in favor of im-
moderate digging share yet. But as we know at present
that this is not so, we find now that digging is not manuring, and that the story of the vineyard is but a story.
The stirring of the soil is useful, as it permits the air to
penetrate the soil and to assist in the formation of carbonic
acid; it opens also the soil to a more thorough influence
of the rain. In digging, the greatest care must be used
not to go so deep as to touch the roots; for, to remove the
soil from the fibrous roots, would be equal to a destruction
of the whole crop. In vineyards covered with debris of
rocks, no digging can take place, except in the spring,
when the vineyard is either manured or only stirred.
Very frequently the vines are manured in the spring, in

order to make use of the manure collected during the winter. It would be better to manure in the fall, and to preserve the winter manure in heaps for the following year. But at present manure is so scarce that such a course cannot be thought of. To pay people for digging, is an expense which does not enrich the soil. In a rational culture of the soil this expense will be reduced to that which is unavoidably necessary; the money saved in this way is better employed in buying fertilizing materials for improving the soil.

In some books, nice distinctions are made in regard to different kinds of manures, such as hen, sheep, hog, pigeon, and other manures. Of one it is said, that it is too dry, another, again, too moist. All such distinctions amount to nothing and are meaningless. If the manures are " Japanized " before their application, they are all equally good, because all animals live on the same constituents of the plants.

THE AGE OF THE VINEYARD.

In our climates the age of the vineyard is, as a rule, twenty-five or thirty, and in some localities fifteen or twenty years; then the vines commence to be unproductive, and a new plantation causes a loss of four or five years. Bronner describes, as early as twenty-six years ago, in his work " Viticulture on the Rhine," No. 3, p. 33, this gradual failing of the vine. He says : " The vines produce but a few grapes ; although they bloom like other vigorous ones, yet they have not power to make fine wood ; they turn yellow and sickly, and look at last as if their pith had been killed by frost. Many vineyards of this kind, especially towards Mentz, (he speaks of the vineyards at Hochheim,) on the westerly side of the place, show such a sickly weakness ; no stimulant nor any manure can restore them to their former vigor. Such enfeebled vines may be considered as a cancer in the household; they are a dead capital, the interest from which, the expected crops, the owner loses, and on which he bestows besides, annually, unprofitable labor. Is not," Bronner continues, " this short life to be ascribed to the fact that the soil has been used during many centuries for the same purpose, so that it is now exhausted?" But what has been abstracted from it ? Hœrter thinks, that there is a want of humus, (vegetable mould, muck,) which is, according to him, the soul of the vegetable kingdom. If such soil is leeched out, and the liquid is a colorless fluid, then it is exhausted and unproductive. But Bronner observes correctly that the vines do not grow better after an application of humus, and that they thrive luxuriantly on the other hand in pure argillaceous marl, which does not contain the slightest trace of humus. " For," he says, " it is an established fact that vines grow best in soil on which vines have never before grown, in a virgin soil, never worked before; in such soil they reach also a greater age."

" I," says Bronner, " have endeavored to investigate the matter in the vineyards; I have called natural philosophy and chemistry to my assistance; I have conversed about it with scientific men; but no explanation is satisfactory to me as yet without resorting to hypothetical phrases."

This excellent man felt, twenty-six years ago, that all explanations then in vogue were unsatisfactory, and yet, on the following page, he seems inclined to assent to the view that the roots of the plants excrete matter injurious to their own growth. What are the present teachings of science in this respect ? *We know that no stimulants exist for plants, but only nourishment.* We know that the plants do not excrete anything injurious to themselves, that cannot be changed again into carbonic acid by rotting. We know that the whole doctrine of humus is nothing but error and deception. The only cause of the premature death of the vines, which is true and perfectly

sufficient, lies in the exhaustion of the soil of mineral constituents, and in too short pruning. The reasons given
by Bronner prove this. The soil may be rendered incapa-
ble of producing vines as of producing clover. After a
few years the roots of the vine penetrate the soil so deep
that the manure cannot reach them, because it moves
slowly and with difficulty in the soil. So their nourishment can only be taken from the mineral constituents in
their immediate vicinity. *By close pruning we prevent
roots from going deeper in quest of food stored up there.
There exists a mutual action between the formation of
leaves and wood.* The wood fibres, originating from carbonic acid, cannot be formed except by the excretion of
oxygen at the surface of the leaves. The greatest quantity of wood fibre is formed if the vine is not pruned at
all, but suffered to grow at will; *in the same proportion,
also, the root grows, provided that there is a sufficiency of
mineral constituents.* Under this condition, even the
greatest quantity of sugar is formed, but its percentage
in the single cluster does not satisfy us. We diminish, by
pruning, the formation of the absolute amount of sugar,
in order to raise its percentage in the few grapes left. In
this way we diminish the formation of wood and roots,
*and to obtain a very few sweet-clusters, we cripple the vine
by pruning, prevent the root from going deep, and so lay
the foundation of its premature decay.* The vine can
reach the age of 800 years, yet we see it die of old age
under our treatment after the short life of twenty-five
years. To dig deep, or trench, is only effective a few
times, i. e., as long as the lower strata of the soil not yet
exhausted can be dug out and mixed with the others. But
the period of the life of the new vine planted in the place
is successively abridged in each of the following attempts,
and ends necessarily by the relinquishment of the land if
the mineral ingredients taken from below are not restored
again below. Manuring is useful for an indefinite period

if only plants, the roots of which spread near the surface, are cultivated. That is the reason why mowing land, and a wheat field may be kept constantly productive, but not a field sown to Lucerne, a vineyard, or a forest. Experience has proved abundantly that the field of Lucerne, when giving out, cannot be restored, even by manuring it most abundantly.

The mineral constituents of the plants are contained in the soil in an insoluble form, or they are changed to such a form by combining with other constituents of the soil, if they are mixed with it in a solution. For instance, sulphate of potash cannot filter through the soil when dissolved in water, nor can phosphate of lime, when dissolved by carbonic acid; they remain in the uppermost stratum, and nearly pure water filters through. If the humus does contain minerals, it is excellent, but without them, not worth a farthing. Nothing grows in peat, nothing in brown coal, both being nearly pure humus, except they make ashes containing potash, which is hardly ever the case. All this leads us necessarily to the fundamental truth already stated in the above, that viticulture can, in the future, only be based on manuring with minerals, and that without them it will disappear in the course of time, as has already been the case in the plains of middle Germany and in the Rhine country, if it cannot be carried on by manuring with minerals. But how can this be effected? Science will assist also in that, because she alone can give aid. Road-dust from granite, syenite, phorphyry, etc., will, as has been already mentioned, be exported as an article of trade and conveyed by the railroads, which diminish so much the formation of road-dust. The few roads yet used for carts and carriages, will be considered as the mills which pulverize the rocks without extra labor. Pure feldspar will be very much preferred; from the proceeds from the sale of the dust the roads can be kept in good order, still leaving a margin of profit. If the percentage of potash is the same in different rocks, the softest will be preferred; different granites will be analyzed, in order to find such as contain the greatest percentage of potash. Perhaps granite will be heated, thrown into cold water, and pulverized in mills, to take from nature by force what she is taking from us daily through the plants. Enormous quantities of potash are contained in the ocean. In Southern France, thousands of tons of potash salts are sent to the markets; they are obtained from the lyes of the salt yards. The water of the ocean contains more than one thousandth part of its weight of chloride of potassium. In the water of the Dead Sea is contained one and one-third per cent. of chloride of potassium, consequently ten times more than in the water of the ocean. The trachytes of the Eifel contain four and one-half per cent.; the phorphyry of Kreuznach, five and one-half per cent.; that of Freiburg seven and a half per cent.; the phronolite of Hohenkræhen even twenty-four per cent. of potash. This shows that enormous quantities of such materials, as we need so much for growing plants, are accumulated. Science will find and make known the localities where they are to be found; technical art will find the means of making them available.

THE RISING SAP IN THE VINE.

More than a hundred years ago an English clergyman, by the name of Stephen Hales, made an experiment to measure by a column of water or quicksilver the force of the rising sap in the vine. I am not in possession of his original work, yet the experiment is mentioned in many books; but I do not find that anybody has ever either repeated or confirmed the experiment, so that at last, on account of the length of time, doubts were raised whether it were so or not. Hales inserted the cut end of a cane in a glass tube, bent in the form of the letter S. The sap issuing from the wound rose twenty-one feet high.

4

Hales then filled the tube with quicksilver, which rose to a height of thirty-two inches. Out of curiosity I repeated this experiment in the year 1849, and found that the results obtained by Hales were perfectly correct. I have not published anything about it, but I think this a good opportunity to communicate here, verbatim, the results as noted down in my memorandum book.

"On the 16th of April I repeated the frequently mentioned experiment of Hales in regard to the rising of the sap in the vine. At first I arranged glass tubes for the sap to rise in them; but I had to give this up because the sap filled the glass tubes very soon, and I was prevented by the wall on which the vine (Chasselas,) grew, from making them longer.

"Then the apparatus, represented in Fig. 12, was arranged. It consisted of a glass bottle closed with a cork, which was tied firmly to the glass, so that it could not be forced out nor even moved. The cork was perforated with two holes, in one of which a small glass tube, bent at a right angle, was inserted; in the

Fig. 12.

other, a glass tube, three feet long, which nearly touched the bottom. The cane was fresh cut and connected with the small glass tube by means of an India rubber tube, enlarged to receive the cane, and then surrounded by thick strips of linen. The bottle contained quicksilver an inch deep; the remaining space was filled with water, without a bubble of air.

The rising took place in the following manner:

April 16, A. M., 1849,	9 o'clock	45 min.,	1"—
" " "	10 "	10 "	3" 10"''
" " "	10 "	30 "	4" 10"''
" " "	11 "	— "	7"—
" " "	11 "	30 "	7" 4"''
" " "	12 "	— "	7" 6"''
April 16, P. M., 1849,	12 "	43 "	8" 7"''
" " "	2 "	9 "	11"—
" " "	3 "	47 "	12"—
" " "	7 "	— "	13"—
" " "	9 "	45 "	15—
April 17, A. M., 1849,	8 "	15 "	19" 3"''

then it commenced falling again.

According to the spec. gr. of the quicksilver of 13.57, the height of nineteen and a quarter inches of the quicksilver is equal to a pressure of water of 26.12. The quicksilver did not, in my experiment, rise so high as in Hales', but high enough to confirm the facts. This phenomenon remains yet unexplained. Neither the law of capillary attraction nor endosmosis furnish the least means of explanation, although both have so frequently been resorted to. The cause of the sap rising seems to lie in the whole length of the cane. The fact that the uppermost eyes push always most vigorously, agrees with it.

The liquid is, according to my researches, very weak in constituents. One litre gave only 2.43 grammes of dry matter, or 0.243 per cent. ; this, reduced to ashes, weighed only 0.65 grammes, or 0.065 per cent. ingredients of the ashes. The ashes showed a very feeble alkaline reaction. It contained lime, and I could trace a little phosphoric acid by molybdanic acid. The liquid, mixed with sugar, does not ferment. It contains, therefore, no albuminous matter, and remains perfectly clear by boiling. The loss of matter, therefore, which the vine sustains by bleeding, is of very little account, except we consider it unnatural

that the vine should indulge in the satisfaction of its tendency to raise the sap so high. It is a ridiculous supersti-
tion that this liquid serves a good purpose as an eye water.

THE GRAPE DISEASE.

In the year 1845, a fungus originated at Margate, in
England, in a vinery for forcing grapes. It is related that
it escaped through a broken window light, and commenced
its destructive travel over Europe and the adjoining parts
of the world. It attacks unripe berries, covering them
with a coat resembling flour; its roots penetrate the skin
of the berry, destroys thereby its structure, so that it cannot grow any more. As the sap continues flowing to it, it
cracks from want of expansibility, dries up, and decays.
It creeps on the berry along the peduncle to the shoots
and leaves, covering the whole vine with a white film, except the woody parts of it. Single spores, carried by wind
or insects to distant points, create a new source of infection from which it spreads again by creeping, so that,
by these two ways of dissemination, in a short time, the
largest trellises of vines are destroyed. The fungus in
question belongs to the genus of the *Oïdiums*, resembling
egg-shaped pearls, as transparent as glass, which are, as it
were, strung on a thread; when they are detached and
separated, they sprout and make roots. Of these Oïdiums
many species were known long ago, but they were of no
importance compared with that in question, because they
appeared only now and then, attacking only wild plants
of no value. The grape fungus, however, spreads so
rapidly, and the plant attacked by it is of so great importance, that it attracted general attention. The question
might be asked here why this fungus was not observed
earlier. We cannot answer it from history. We know,
however, from the recent investigations of Darwin and
others, that the species of plants and animals are not constant; they are subject to continual changes caused by ex-

ternal conditions and circumstances. Although not a single case of *generatio spontanea s. equivoca*, (immediate creation within the historical period,) has been established or proved, yet we recognize the fact that beings, already in existence, may be very much changed by external conditions, especially those lowest organisms with their simple organs. The nature of the Oïdiums is changed by the nature of the body on which they lead their parasitic life. The year 1862 was very productive of different kinds of Oïdiums. I observed in my garden that not only the grapes, but roses, *Thlaspi Bursa-Pastoris*, *Bignonia*, *Catalpa*, cucumbers, squashes, *Lamium album*, peas, and many other plants were attacked. Under the microscope they were so similar in form, that they all might have been regarded as the same. It is true, they showed little differences in the form, yet they did not necessarily establish a difference of the species; it is very probable that the same spore has a different development on the leaves of the cucumber, or *Bignonia*, from that which it would have on the tender leaves of the pea. In this way, the spore of an Oïdium, grown on another plant, may have settled on the berry of a grape vine in a warm, moist glass house, and its nature may have been changed so much, that it was now especially fit to grow on grapes. Consequently, it is not in the least remarkable that the grape disease has not made its appearance earlier, but only after a new species had been called into existence by favorable circumstances, a species especially fit to live on the juice of unripe grapes. So the disease came into existence and has not as yet disappeared. There is reason to believe that the spores of the Oïdium may remain dormant during the winter, on the infected canes and buds. This is proved by the fact that the disease re-appears regularly in southern countries, and that its recurrence in northern, colder countries, is irregular and sporadic. With us, the disease seems to be destroyed by a severe winter; for

many cases are known in which it did not re-appear in localities where it was very prevalent the year before. In
countries enjoying mild winters, like Madeira, Tyrol, and
Italy, its re-appearance may be predicted almost to a day.
There is also a difference in regard to its appearance. In
the South, it is frequently observed before the time of blossoming; with us, not until the berries have attained the size
of small peas. The warm months of April and May, in
1862, developed the spores so early that the disease had
already spread to a great extent in the beginning of July.

At the first appearance of this Oïdium, which was called
by Berkeley *Oïdium Tuckeri*, those whose vineyards
were affected by it, were driven to despair. The description of it given by Mr. de Comini, the owner of a farm
at Botzen, is really awful. Year after year the whole crop
was lost, families sank into poverty, and emigration and
seizure of their property followed.

The results of the experiments to counteract this calam-
ity, were slow, and centered in the view entertained that
pulverized sulphur, sprinkled over the vines, was a never
failing specific. At first, the operation was performed in
a defensive way; only the clusters attacked by the fungus, were sprinkled. Afterwards it was thought better to
use the sulphur as a preventive; the whole vine was
sprinkled with sulphur to prevent the disease. At last,
experience established the fact, that it is necessary to ap-
ply the sulphur four or five times, to kill the spores, and to
prevent the disease from spreading.

In the beginning of July, in 1862, I noticed for the first
time on a trellis a spot affected with the disease; it had
never appeared before in the same garden. At that time
my garden contained several thousand feet of trellis; I
saw at once the difficulty, amounting almost to an impos-
sibility of staying the disease by sprinkling the leaves and
bunches, for some of the trellises were from sixteen to
twenty feet high, and not accessible without the use of a

ladder. Thinking over all the experiments made to combat the evil, I saw that they were mostly only prophylactic, (preventive.) I concluded, therefore, to proceed at once in a defensive way, and to destroy the spores as soon as they originated. The result showed that this was much easier than it seemed to be at first. The diseased spot was thoroughly cleansed; all bunches seized with the disease, beyond the possibility of curing them, were broken off, and the leaves and branches severely beaten with towels and brushwood.

Then the diseased spot with its surroundings was very frequently examined, and all new attacks of the disease instantly annihilated. This was effected in the following manner: I carried a deep box filled with flowers of sulphur, around the neck, by means of a cord, so that I had it before me, in which a common hair brush, an inch thick, was kept. In examining the clusters, great facility of recognizing the disease is very soon acquired, so that there is not the least doubt about it. Especially the small berries which are not developed, because they are not fertilized, are seized when they are not larger than a pin's head. These appear as if powdered white, while everything else around them is in order yet. Where there is such a berry, there is generally, also, a small empty space by which the infection is retarded. Such a cluster is then taken in the hollow of the left hand, then brushed powerfully with the brush, not charged with sulphur, and then dusted over by means of the same brush with sulphur. A spot, so treated, is always saved. The sooner the examination of the vines commences, the easier it is to accomplish the purpose. Oftentimes many days elapse before a new infection takes place. In a large garden, of three acres area, with vines planted everywhere, it required but an hour every day to arrest the evil.

Sometimes I found twenty spots affected, sometimes but one, and had the disease not already spread so much before I noticed it, the task would have been still easier. *The disease always attacks the bunches first, and only appears on the leaves and branches later ;* if it is destroyed on the berries it does not reach the leaves. When the bunches begin to ripen, they are in less danger than the leaves and green shoots. The bunches so treated ripened perfectly on vines, of which every leaf was affected.

The protection is, therefore, to be confined to the clusters, as it is impossible to treat leaves and shoots in a like manner. In a cluster saved, the object of the labor is before us ; it is not so near and immediate in the leaves and shoots, the number of which is much larger. The offensive (prophylactic) treatment causes under all circumstances the same amount of labor, the defensive only in proportion to what is really saved.

The first traces of the disease appear, as stated, always on the unripe cluster. The disease does not spread, nor do the leaves or the green shoots suffer when the fungus is destroyed there.

There is no place for the spores of the Oïdium, but on the green shoots, which will be canes in the fall by changing their green color into brown. This fact was proven by the experiments of Mr. de Comini. In November, he cut off infected canes, which was evident from the dark spots on them, and kept them in a warm room, in pots, having horse-manure and sods at the bottom. After the lapse of seven weeks, the fungus appeared on those dark spots, covering, in a short time, the whole cane. It is therefore very important to watch the vines carefully in the spring in order to destroy the fungus as soon as it makes its appearance ; this will very much diminish its spreading.

[From the above statement and description of Dr. Mohr, it is evident that the Oïdium as prevalent in Europe is either different from that which attacks the American va rieties, or modified and changed, to a certain degree, by atmospheric influences. The grape vine disease, at least here, at the East, always attacks the leaves first, and the clusters only later, if they are attacked at all. It is well known that Dr. Engelmann, of St. Louis, and other naturalists of this country, consider the European and American Oïdium as two different species, and maintain, besides, that there is a second species also in America. Be this as it may, it is an established fact that flowers of sulphur is a specific against the disease prevalent in America as well as that in Europe. To destroy the spores in the spring before the buds swell, it is beneficial to sprinkle them thoroughly by means of a garden syringe, with the following mixture, recommended by Mr. Neubert, of Leipsic, the scientific vine grower.

Eight and a half ounces of common salt, and four ounces of saltpetre must be dissolved in 36 ounces of water; add to the solution, 10 drops of oil of Rosemary, and 10 drops of oil of Lavender. Take one part of the solution and use it with 100 or 120 parts of water. It must be vigorously stirred before using it, on account of the essential oils which otherwise would easily separate from it.

The trellises, posts and walls, must also be thoroughly sprinkled as well as the vines. As soon as the leaves expand they must be dusted all over with flowers of sulphur, then again when they blossom, a third time when the berries are as large as peas, and lastly, when they begin to color. This, of course, is a prophylactic treatment; but as the berries are attacked later than the leaves, if at all, it can not be otherwise. The effect of the sulphuration is very powerful. Flowers of sulphur also keep the thrips in check, an enemy of the grape vine that grows every day more formidable.

The vines may be dusted by means of a brush; yet it is difficult by means of it to dust the underside of the leaves.

4*

The bellows invented in France, by Mr. De La Vergue, (figure 13,) is the most convenient instrument for dusting all parts of the vine thoroughly, especially the underside of the leaves. Several years ago I imported a number

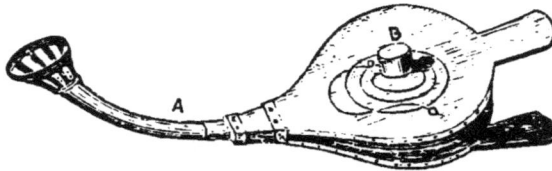

Fig. 13.

of them from France, at great expense and loss, for patterns to have them manufactured here. They can be obtained from the Messrs. Woodward, editors of the Horticulturist, who have them always on hand.

There is another instrument, called, in Germany, the "Grape-vine Torch." It consists of a conical duster made of tin, the bottom of which is perforated with a great number of small holes. Sometimes the holes are made larger, so that pieces of woolen yarn (worsted) can be passed through them, leaving space enough for the sulphur to be shaken through, and to spread evenly by the pieces of woolen yarn which project several inches from the bottom. Such a duster must be about eight or ten inches long, and at the bottom about four inches or four and a half in diameter. There must, of course, be a cover to it to prevent the sulphur from falling out. Figure 14 illustrates the grape vine torch, with a portion of the side removed to show the interior arrangement.

Fig. 14.

This instrument has the same disadvantage as a brush, because the underside of the leaves can only with difficulty be dusted over by means of it.

The sulphuration ought to be performed in the middle of the day when the sun shines; should a sudden rain wash the sulphur off, it must immediately be repeated as soon as the weather becomes dry.

It would be useless to mention here other remedies for destroying that terrible disease; for instance, three parts of coal tar mixed with ninety-seven parts of sand or dry soil. Some of this compound laid about the vines is said to prevent the disease; but sulphur, if properly applied, never fails to prevent or destroy it.—*Translator.*]

TREATMENT OF VINES INJURED BY FROST.

In our northern climates, the wood of the vine suffers during winters that are very cold. No buds push in the spring, and the wood dries up in the course of the summer. It is true it does not happen frequently, yet it happens sometimes. To prevent this, the vines pruned in the fall are covered with soil. This is the rule in the east of Germany; in the west, on the Rhine, it is not customary, because truly dangerous winters are of too rare occurrence to warrant the same laborious work annually.

Vines injured by frost are, in this region, cut off just above ground; but this operation is injurious and faulty in the highest degree. The roots not having suffered from frost send up in the spring an abundance of sap, which flows out of the large wound. This flow of the sap continues not unfrequently for a month, and consequently the young shoots are lessened and retarded. These young shoots cannot ripen their wood in the course of the summer, so that in the following winter they suffer again from the frost. The treatment of a vine injured by frost must therefore be entirely changed from this. The injured vines must not be pruned at all, in order to prevent the rising sap from getting wasted; they must be permitted to push just as they are. In this case the number of the pushing eyes is as large as possible, no sap being lost by flowing out.

This causes the shoots to grow vigorously; they can mature their wood in the summer and bear fruit the next year; in the third year all that has been lost by frost may have been replaced by a new growth, and the vine may have attained its former size. In this way only one crop is lost.

If the vine was pruned in the fall, nothing is cut off after the frost in the spring ; the young shoots, which appear in large numbers, must be suffered to grow until they are four or five feet long. Then the weakest of them are removed, without injuring the strong ones, in order to make them grow more vigorously. Pinching the laterals must be entirely omitted until at pruning in the fall. The eyes of the young shoots may all, in the course of the summer, be sufficiently well developed for producing blossoms, because no sap in this case is used for nourishing fruit. The pruning in the fall must be very moderate, and confined to the removal of the laterals.

The vine does not suffer from covering it with soil; it is not even injured by inundation. A small vineyard adjoining my farm is almost every year flooded by the Moselle, during ten or fourteen days; it has never suffered from it, and seems to do better than others. There are vineyards on the Rhine, between Coblenz and Bingen, which are flooded nearly every year, without suffering in the least. The vine may suffer in the spring from late frosts coming after leaves and blossoms have appeared. The warmer the spring, and the more advanced the shoots, the greater is the danger. In this respect the cold days, from the twelfth to the fourteenth of May, are well known and dreaded; they are generally called the cold saints, *Pancratius, Servatius* and *Bonifacius.* It is a well established fact, corroborated by many years' experience, that at that time a cold storm from the north visits the middle of Europe, often destroying in a single night the hopes of a whole year. The cause of the phenomenon is as yet unknown. It is not always coincident with the days mentioned; for it may come one or two weeks earlier, or a few days later. In our region this storm was in a certain year experienced on the 21st day of April; in another (1854), on the 24th of April, not injuring the yet undeveloped shoots of the vine, while the plums and pears then in blossom suffered severely. Nothing has been proposed or attempted against such cold storms except filling the air with smoke from slowly burning brushwood, sods and moist straw. Smoke makes the air less transparent, and so prevents the warmth from radiating. Although the prospects for the crop of a whole year are at stake, and, in consequence of it, the vintner's means of living, yet smoking is rarely, and nowhere regularly, resorted to. The danger is greatest about an hour and a half or two hours before sunrise; but at that time man is overpowered by sleep. The difficulty of leaving the bed and remaining in the open air during a long cold night will always be in the way of its practice, and will be the cause of neglecting to save the vines in the way mentioned. Fatalism is a convenient belief; it permits one to remain in bed while it is freezing hard. Such systems have always many followers.

In clear nights, a broad cold current of air descends slowly from the summits of the mountains; the direction of it can be easily ascertained by the motion of the smoke from a pipe or a cigar. Smoking fires should therefore regularly be built, just above the vineyard, on the highest spot between the mountain and the vineyard. Should there be a high wind, there is hardly any danger, because it surrounds and warms again the parts of the vine cooled by radiation. If there is no wind and the smoke rises in a straight column, it cannot be of any use. To observe all these things in a dark night, is not an easy matter.

Smoking fires will long remain in the books, where they are strongly recommended, before they will be resorted to in practical life.

IMPLEMENTS.

The implements absolutely necessary for the management of the vine are, first : garden shears, and secondly, a knife.

Good garden shears are at present so well known that a description of them would be useless.

The pruning knife, which may without inconvenience be carried in the pocket, was, before the introduction of correctly made shears, the only implement of the gardener. It has been in a great measure superseded by shears, because nearly all the work may be done with those equally well and with greater dispatch. At present the pointed form, Figure 15, is alone recommended in horticultural books, while knives, sharply curved at their ends, such as were formerly used, are not thought much of. It seems to me that there is no good cause for overpraising the former and undervaluing the latter. The pointed knife does not cut, except the blade is pressed powerfully against the branch.

Fig. 15.

In order to be able to do this, the knife must be grasped as shown in Figure 16; this, however, requires a great strength in the hand, when the cut is made with the point, the part of the knife which is thinnest and best fitted for cutting.

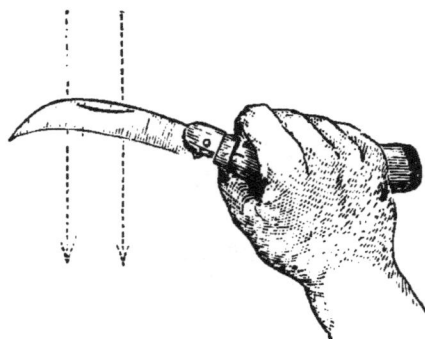

Fig. 16.

If the knife is curved at the point, as in the old form,

the greatest resistance is in a direct line with the hand and arm, (fig. 17,) and the cut becomes more of a pull than in the other form, in which it is a pressure from the side.

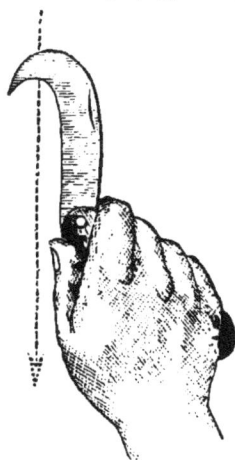

Yet a drawing cut is the most effective of all, because the muscles of the upper part of the arm come into play. In using the knife in this way, the drawing would pull it out of the hand if this were not counteracted by a strong grasp. The exertion made in preventing the knife from slipping out of the hand is a real waste, because it does not co-operate in cutting. The handle must therefore, at its end, be so arranged, by an upward flat bend,

Fig. 17.

that the solid part of the hand below the little finger may rest upon it. When the hand is only so much closed that the knife may not fall out, the drawing of the arm accomplishes the cut without any waste of power. The cutting with such a knife is much more effective, and may be continued much longer without fatigue. It is very convenient for a gardener not to be compelled to open the knife every time he needs it, but to carry it open in a case in the pocket, as sailors are accustomed to do.

The knife is still more convenient when the blade is bent a little on the back towards the handle, as represented in Figure 18.

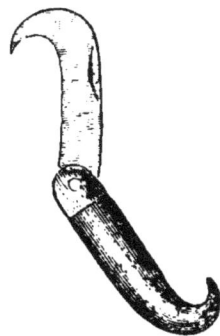

Fig. 18.

In this case the blade is not movable, and the knife must be carried in a case. The handle is made of two pieces of wood, united by rivets with the prolongation of the blade. The blade need only be half as long as that of the common pruning knives, the lower part of which is never used for cutting. But the length of the handle must be independent of the length of the blade; it must correspond to the size of the hand of a man; that is, it must be four and a half inches (about 120 m.m.) long, and nearly an inch (10 lines or 32 m.m.) thick.

The proportions of many good knives in the market are faulty, the handles being too small, and the blades also small.

The size of the blade is regulated by the work for which it is intended ; the handle, however, must fit the hand, which is always the same. Frequently, the springs are too strong, so that the knife cannot be opened without using great power; it is sometimes even dangerous.

In the shears, the axis on which the arms move is fastened in a wrong way, so that the screw is apt to get loose in using them. The cause for this wrong construction may lie in the gardeners themselves ; if they have no clear insight into the matter, they cannot give good advice to the manufacturers; consequently, faulty arrangements continue to be handed down from one to another. Without increasing the labor and cost, those implements might be made much better.

Even many horticultural books show that their authors do not understand the advantages of shears over knives. They concede that by using shears the work is done with greater dispatch, yet they say that the knife is better. The reason why shears deserve to be preferred to the knife, lies in the fact that shears carry, aside from the cutting knife, the resistance along with them, so that the stress upon the trellis or the root and vine below the cut is easily avoided. Shears have not only a knife, but also another arm towards which the cutting is directed. If the shears are turned a little in cutting, they bruise the branch as little as the knife ; for the more easily the cleft opens for the cutting blade, the less pressure is exerted on the other arm. In cutting with shears it does not matter whether we cut high in the air, or low, near the ground ; in using the knife we have always to consider in what direction we may find the resistance in order to cut in that which is opposite to it.

We will give here some hints for cutters in regard to the best arrangement for knives and shears.

The blades of garden knives of the modern pointed form, Figure 19, ought to project only two inches beyond the handle. The best cast steel should be used for them ; they ought to be tempered yellow, but blue near the handle. The rivets, on which the blade moves, ought to be $\frac{2}{12}$ thick, made of steel wire, and the points rounded. They must not be fastened by riveting, but should be driven into the handle under a strong friction, but the blade must move freely and easily. All blades of a given number should be of the same dimensions ; this enables the buyer to purchase two or three blades which may easily be exchanged by taking out the rivet. The blade should not have a projection at the end ; it ought to have a sharp edge its whole length. The handle, being as long as the hand is broad, ought to be bent backwards on its lower extremity for the hand to rest upon it ; a little projection on the back, about an inch below the rivet, is very useful in holding the knife firmly ; this projection will go in between the fore and the middle finger of the right hand.

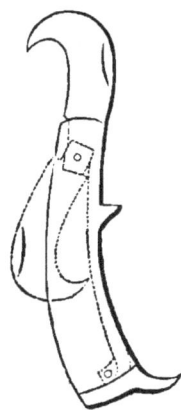

Fig. 19.

Curved blades, Figure 20, need not be longer than 1 inch and $\frac{2}{3}$; their sharp edge must extend along their whole length ; otherwise they do not differ from straight knives. The springs must be good, but not too strong ; the wooden handle ought to be painted red, to enable one

Fig. 20.

to find them easily when lost, as the common brown color of the handles makes it difficult to see them on the ground.

In shears the pivot is fitted in a square hole of that arm on which there is a nut with a screw to fasten the two arms together. Very frequently this nut gets loose. To avoid this, two nuts are put on the screw. The lowermost being larger, projects considerably from the uppermost. It has two incisions opposite each other, to receive a screw-driver, which is so arranged that it fits them. The second nut, the so called counternut, is screwed down to the first, on which it is held in place by friction.

PROPER TIME FOR THE WORK TO BE PERFORMED ON THE VINE.

We have already, when we had occasion, pointed out the best time for the work to be performed on the vine and given the reasons for it. At present we shall explain the matter fully.

The pruning of the vine ought to be done in autumn, immediately after the fall of the leaf. By it, the vine is reduced to smaller dimensions, it is easier to keep it in the right condition during the winter, and the wood so removed may be cut up and mixed with the manure. Immediately after pruning, the vine ought to be manured in the manner described above.

When the vine is not to be manured, the pieces of the canes are cut up, and the leaves are placed where they will decay. It is a general custom to go over the vines in gardens and vineyards again in the spring, to prune a little, and then to tie them immediately. This procedure is altogether erroneous, because it renders regular pinching impossible; that is the reason that the pinching is omitted in every vineyard. It is advisable to perform the operation of the last pruning, the pinching and tying at the same time; by this the second labor is saved. For this purpose nothing is done on the vine in the spring, until the time of the powerful rising of the sap has passed, after which the vine may be cut without bleeding. As nobody can tell which buds will produce blossoms, it is necessary to wait until they appear.

With us (on the Rhine), the vine blossoms within a month, commencing after the first week in June. The last pruning of the vine, together with pinching, must therefore be done a little before or after blossoming. Then all blossom buds are developed, and the shoots, which will bear fruit, can be selected. Up to that time the vine is suffered to swing untied about the poles, or to hang on the trellis. There is nothing so easily injured as the eye of the vine that has just started. It is broken off when slightly touched with the arm, or when the branch receives a push. When the vines are pruned and tied in March, it is at a time when the eyes have just pushed, and when they are easily injured.

Moreover, the leader for the year cannot well be distinguished or chosen at that time. When, on the contrary, the last pruning and pinching are done in the first half of June, it is easy to select the shoots for next year's bearing; also the shoots destitute of blossoms can be seen. The vine is open and expanded before the vintner.

Commencing at the base of the vine, the vintner selects the shoots intended for canes the next year. He is careful that there are not too many left on any one part of the stem, but that the whole number is equally distributed over the different heads of the stem; then he proceeds with his work in an upward direction, pinching all shoots which show blossoms at two leaves beyond the uppermost cluster, and removing their laterals or the buds in the axils of their leaves. Should there be a cane without any shoots showing blossoms, it is to be cut off above the lowermost shoot.

Then nothing is left on the vine but the shoots intended
for canes, and the pinched shoots with blossoms.

It is obvious that the clusters on such a vine must be
more perfect and better than on vines of which the shoots
that do not bear are left to grow; there will be at
last a profusion of useless wood and leaves to be cut off
in the fall. As soon as the shoots not bearing are removed, the shoot for bearing canes, as well as those pinched, develops rapidly, growing so vigorously and strong, and
maturing its wood so well, that the results of this pruning
and pinching will be far more favorable than would
have been the case had they been treated in the common
way. The early tying in March prevents the vintner from
performing these operations, because it would imply the
necessity of cutting the vines loose again, in order to have
free access to all parts. In this way the labor of the first
tying would be lost. I have had the experience, that the
vines of a vineyard, tied before development, had to be
loosened in order to pinch and to remove unfruitful shoots.
A great deal of wood had to be removed, which caused
the rest to develop, and grow the more vigorously. Pinching and removing unfruitful shoots requires some knowledge; therefore only experienced persons are to be entrust-
ed with this operation, while others, receiving lower wages,
may be employed to tie them up. To recapitulate: my
rule is not to do any thing to the vine, either in the vineyard or in the garden, before all the blossoms are visible
and developed, and then to remove unfruitful shoots, and
to perform pinching and tying at the same time.

I see now, clearly, why vignerons are so much opposed
to pinching. If they do not discontinue their custom of
tying in March, they of course cannot do anything to
them in June. The first step would be, to dispense with
the operations performed in March; but that would be

conflicting too much with the habits and prejudices of the vignerons, which are paramount to every thing else. Besides, the spring work done to the vine, when deferred till June, is profitable in a pecuniary point of view. In March, plowing and sowing are to be done in the fields; therefore help is always scarce. In the beginning of June, there is an ebb in agriculture; grain, potatoes, etc., are growing and do not require any work; mowing is to be done a little later, consequently it is, at this season, easy enough to procure the necessary help. I request intelligent cultivators of the vine to follow my example in pinching and tying late, and then to report the result in public prints.

The effect of removing useless shoots of the vine extends not only over the current, but also over the following year. When unfruitful shoots are suffered to remain, an enormous quantity of shoots and leaves is produced, so that the sap, furnished by the root, is not sufficient to mature them. The consequence is, that a large number of eyes on the shoots intended for canes cannot produce blossoms, but only unfruitful shoots in the following year.

The same is clearly seen in all fruit trees. If all shoots are suffered to grow undisturbed, many fruit trees do not bear for years, that is, not until the root is sufficiently developed for the wood growth, as well as for the formation of blossom buds. But if, in the latter part of the summer, the tops of the twigs are broken off, the lower eyes are changed to fruit buds for the following year. If this pinching is done too early, the lower eyes push, and the object sought is not accomplished. In the vine the period is very late in the season, at which pinching does not excite the lower eyes into growth. The less favorable the weather, the more the vine must be restricted to produce fruit buds in the next year.

CONSTITUENTS OF THE VINE, ACCORDING TO THE PROPORTION IN WHICH THEY ARE DISTRIBUTED IN THE DIFFERENT PARTS.

The inorganic constituents, that is, those contained in the ashes are the same in all parts of the vine, yet in proportions varying a little ; even the ashes from all parts of a certain kind, mixed together, differ a little from those of other kinds. These constituents amount in the canes to from 2.25 to 2.85 per cent., in the small Burgundy to 3.692 per cent., if the boiling point of the water is taken to determine their dryness. The must, without exsiccation, contains in unripe, blue grapes 0.259 per cent., in ripe ones 0.34 per cent., from another place 0.409 per cent. of ashes.

The skins of the little Burgundy, dried at the temperature of 212°, contain 3.737 per cent., of the Schoenfeilner 4.321 per cent.; the seeds of the small Burgundy, dried at 212°, 2.776 per cent., those of the Schoenfeilner 2.882 per cent. of ashes. In these ashes, potash and phosphoric acid preponderate so much, that we will only mention their relative amount ; otherwise we should have to go into an elaborate detail.

Ashes.	Per cent of Potash.	Per cent. of phosphoric acid.
1) Of the seeds of the blue grapes........	27.868	27.005
2) Of the seeds of white grapes..........	29.454	21.054
3) Of wood from canes (little Burgundy).	37.309	9.587
4) Of the skins of blue grapes...........	44.656	7.055
5) Of the must of white grapes..........	62.745	17.044
6) Of the must of ripe blue grapes........	65.043	16.578
7) Of the must of unripe blue grapes.....	66.334	15.378
8) Of the must of ripe blue grapes........	71.852	14.073
(Plaenermergel.)		

In the first column, the constituents are arranged according to the increasing amount of potash ; in the second column the amount of phosphoric acid is decreasing nearly in the same ratio ; the proportion of phosphoric acid, contained in the must, is different from that contained in the body of the vine. But in the four kinds of must phosphoric acid decreases also, in the same ratio in which the amount of potash increases. This circumstance is too regular to be accidental; but its significance is, as yet, unknown. It is evident from this that the greatest amount of potash and phosphoric acid is carried out of the vineyard along with the wine.

The smallest amount of potash, that is, from 3 to 5 per cent., is contained in the must; a larger amount, *i.e.*, from 20 to 21 per cent. in the ashes of the skins; a still greater amount, *i.e.*, from 32 to 35 per cent. in the ashes of the seed; the greatest, however, *i.e.*, from 36 to 43½ per cent. in the ashes of canes. The amount of soda is, on the whole, small, viz. : 1 per cent. in the ashes of must, and 3 per cent. in those of canes ; that of sulphuric acid is in the ashes of the vine, from 2 to 3 per cent., in those of the must 5 per cent.

The organic constituents are distributed in the following proportion :

Old wood and that from canes contain *starch*. If wood be cut in small pieces and boiled in water, the liquid turns blue by adding a solution of iodine. Unripe wood does not contain starch. The peduncles of the grape contain some of it in the middle of the summer, but not afterwards, because it goes back into the vine. The berry is the only part of the vine which contains sugar ; it is not found in any other. In the juice of the ripe berry there are tartaric and malic acid, bitartrate of potash, and vegetable albumen, but no tannic acid, either in white or blue grapes.

Free acid decreases in the ratio in which the grape matures, until it reaches that amount which is proportionate to the variety or the temperature of the year. After having reached this point the acid seems to again increase a little. If the free acid is considered as crystallized tartaric acid, the results of experiments, made in the year 1858, with juice obtained from pressing, were the following:

1. TROLLINGER (Frankenthal, Black Hamburg)—Acid per Mill.
   August 15, entirely unripe,........................... 31.
   August 30, unripe,................................... 31.5
   September 11, not ripe, but colored a little,.......... 28
   October 23, ripe,.................................... 13.
   November 4, ripe,................................... 13.
2. BURGUNDY.
   August 15, entirely unripe,........................... 34.5
   August 30, entirely unripe,........................... 34.
   September 11, part blue and part still green,......... 17.5
   October 15, ripe,.................................... 12.
   October 23, ripe.................................... 9.
   November 4, ripe,................................... 9.
3. WHITE CHASSELAS.
   August 15, entirely unripe,........................... 34.
   August 30, ripening,................................. 15.
   September 11, eatable, but not quite ripe,........... 11.5
   October 15, perfectly ripe,.......................... 6.
   October 23,.. 6.
   November 4,.. 7.5

These experiments show that the acid in 1 and 2 did not diminish from October 23 to November 4, but that in 3 it increased one and a half thousandths.

The skins of the berries contain tannin. This is shown by boiling them in water and adding a few drops of chloride of iron to the strained liquid, and then a solution of bicarbonate of soda. The color of the liquid is then changed to that of ink. Furthermore the skins of blue grapes contain the coloring matter which, in its composition, is very similar to that of tannin.

The seeds contain a large amount of tannin, and about 5 per cent. of fat oil, but it would cost more to press it out than it is worth. It has a somewhat greenish color, and belongs to the drying oils. If it could be had, it would be useful for many purposes. If the seeds remain in the juice while fermenting, the tannin is exhausted from them, as is the case in red wines. A preparation, containing tannin, can be made from the seeds when extracted with wine or alcohol; it is made use of in the management of wine in the cellar.

The peduncles of the grapes, called combs, contain much tannin as well as free acid. Their taste is acerb and sour. What they impart to the wine, is injurious; neither do they contribute anything to its agreeable taste or to its durability. There are, therefore, three parts containing tannic acid, namely—the skins, the seeds and the combs; it is necessary to take cognizance of this distribution in making wine. Concerning the proportion of the weight of the must and the other parts of the grape, experiments have shown the following:

Berries of the white Chasselas, picked from the combs and powerfully pressed, yield,

Of juice, - - - - - 97 per cent.
Of skins, seeds and solid substance, 3 "

Berries of the blue Burgundy, picked from the combs, yield,

Of juice, - - - - - 94.8 per cent.
Of skins, seeds and solid substance, 5.2 "

Berries of the blue Burgundy, pressed together with the combs, yield,

Of juice, - - - - - 91.8 per cent.
Of combs, skins, seeds and solid
substance, - - - - 9 "   ..

The remains of blue Burgundy grapes, fermented and then pressed, yielded,

Of wine, - - - - - 69.6 per cent.
Of remains, - - - . 30.4 "

From these experiments the great loss in wine, suffered by the vigneron, who generally throws away the pressed husks, is clearly seen; it amounts to 70 per cent. of the weight of the husks. The same is true in regard to the

5

loss of must in the husks of white wine, when they are removed before the fermentation.   There is no press powerful enough to overcome, by mechanical force, this almost
chemical affinity.   They cannot be effectually pressed out
until the cells are opened by fermentation.   Raspberries
and gooseberries are similar, in this respect, to grapes.

HINTS

ON THE PROPAGATION AND·GENERAL TREATMENT OF
AMERICAN VARIETIES.

BY

THE TRANSLATOR.

———•••———

PROPAGATION OF THE GRAPE VINE.

As the propagation of the Continental varieties of the
vine is attended with so little difficulty, that it cannot be
compared with that of the American species and their
varieties, Dr. Mohr's excellent work would not, in this
respect, give satisfaction to the American reader. To
make additions and alterations would have been very in-
convenient; we have, therefore, preferred to omit Dr.
Mohr's chapter on propagation, altogether, and to insert
here a brief description of the methods used in this country
for the propagation of the native vine, and practiced by
ourselves. Growers of the grape, on a large scale, will
resort to more extensive and complicated arrangements.
They will find a detailed description of them in *Fuller's
Grape Culturist*, a thoroughly practical work on the management of the vine.

99

I.—BY LAYERS.

Layering is an easy and certain way to obtain young plants, and consists in bending a cane or a green shoot down to the ground, and covering it with soil. The part so buried will be found well rooted in the fall.

To make a layer of a cane (old wood), make a little ditch four or six inches deep and long enough to receive the cane. This must, of course, be made near the vine, but so that the roots of it may not be injured. If this cannot be avoided, the smallest roots being so near the surface of the ground, it is better to make the ditch at a little distance from the vine, and to bury only a part of the cane, the rest remaining above ground. Early in the spring, before the buds commence swelling, the cane is laid down into the ditch, and kept in place by.pegs or stones. When the shoots from the cane have grown a few inches, four or six of them are selected and retained; all others are rubbed off, especially those starting from buds on the lower side of the cane. Then fine and rich soil is thrown into the ditch, but not more than about an inch deep at a time. This filling in must be gradually continued in proportion as the shoots grow, until the ditch is full. Too much soil at once, while the shoots are too young and succulent, might cause their decay. *The fewer the plants taken from a cane the stronger they will be.* Fruit bearing is a natural, but exhausting, process; it is, therefore, a bad practice to take fruit from those shoots, as some do. The vine roots so easily that it is not necessary to notch it between the joints, as it is customary in layering other plants.

In the autumn, after the fall of the leaf, the cane is severed from the stem and carefully lifted with a digging fork, so as not to break or mutilate the roots of the young plants. It is then cut into as many pieces as there are plants.

Should a single plant only be desired, the cane may be pruned shorter, bent down into the ditch and covered at once with soil, except the last (highest) bud. This must remain just above ground; therefore, the cane must be bent abruptly upwards at the end of the ditch, and kept in place by a peg or stone. A little stick should indicate the place; otherwise the eye or the shoot from it may inadvertently be destroyed. A layer of this kind made in a basket or box of lattice work, filled with good soil and set in the ground, is easily raised in the fall, and planted, without disturbing it, where it is intended to grow. The roots protruding from the basket or box must be preserved with the utmost care; the receptacle will soon decay, *and a whole year will be gained.* *To recommend, as some do, such box-layer plants for immediate bearing,* is, to say the least, wrong. It is time that those unacquainted with the management of the vine should be cautioned against buying vines of this kind for extravagant prices. Box-layers, if properly managed and planted, are very good, indeed, *but not for immediate bearing.*

Also wood, two years old, roots easily enough, so that a cane which has borne fruit may be used for layering instead of cutting it off in the fall.

Layers may also be made of young green shoots or of the tops of them, in July. All that is necessary is, to cover a part, or the top of a green shoot with soil. I generally put a good-sized stone on it; it keeps the shoot in place, prevents the moisture from evaporating, and equalizes the temperature. Of course, the projecting top must not be injured. Notching, in summer layering, is useful, but not indispensable. If the shoot is too young or the notch too deep or too long, the part above it is apt to wither. From strong shoots, beautiful plants are obtained in this way.

II.—BY CUTTINGS.

Cuttings are pieces of either old wood of the previous year, or of young green wood of the current year, each having one eye at least, mostly two or more. When planted in soil or sand, under suitable conditions, they root very easily, making good plants.

We consider here, first, long cuttings from old wood. In some, especially southern, countries, such as are several feet long, are preferred; in others, such as are a foot or eighteen inches long. At present there is a tendency to make them only six inches long, even shorter, in short-jointed varieties. The wood is preserved in sand, or in common garden soil in a cellar, or at the north side of a building till wanted; it ought to be protected from freezing. At the approach of spring the wood so preserved is cut into small pieces of the length required. The lower cut must be horizontal immediately below a bud; above, it is slanting on the side opposite the bud, but at the distance of about an inch from it. Although it is better to make the lower horizontal cut immediately below an eye, yet this is not absolutely necessary, as the vine quickly roots also from the internodes (the space between two buds). Such a cutting, with a piece of still older wood attached to it, from which the shoot grew, is called a *hammer* cutting. Hammer cuttings were very much preferred by the Romans, and are especially recommended, at present, for the Delaware and other hard-wooded varieties. They are only occasionally obtained, unless the laterals are suffered to grow and to ripen their wood on a cane, which may, in this case, be divided into as many hammer cuttings as there are laterals. The pieces of the cane itself must be half an inch or an inch long.

Cuttings, so prepared, must be tied in bundles, carefully labeled and preserved in sand, till the weather is warm enough, in the middle of April or beginning of May for planting them.

Some put them, about eight or ten days before planting, two or three inches deep in water till the eyes begin to swell. In this way I often succeeded in making Delaware cuttings root in the open air. By accident a number of pieces of that variety, lying in water, had been forgotten; when found, I planted them in clayey soil in the garden, when every one of them grew. I made this accidental experiment known in the "Horticulturist." (See 1863, p. 160).

The planting must be done with care. To make holes with a dibble is certainly a rough practice. Not only are the sides of the hole pressed by it into a solid mass, offering much resistance to the rootlets, but the lower (cut) part of the cutting is too often injured by thrusting it into the hole. It is also in this case difficult to press the soil firmly around the lower part, which is essential.

It is much better to make the holes or ditch with a spade. Long cuttings are planted in a slanting position, in order not to bury their lower ends too deep in the ground. They cannot grow without being excited by the warmth of the soil, imparted by the sun. The upper eye must either be at a level with the surface of the ground, or a quarter of an inch below it. A little sand or moss placed on it will prevent it from drying up before it starts. That such cuttings ought occasionally to be watered, when necessary, does not require any special explanation.

The advantage claimed for cutting more than six inches long, is more specious and imaginary, than real and true. It is true, there are very many nodes in the ground, each of which *may* emit roots; but experience shows that every node of so long a piece of a cane does not emit roots, and so much wood without roots when buried in the ground, is apt to decay. The same object is accomplished, but with certainty and without danger, by layering the cane, growing from a cutting, in one or several successive years.

It is advisable to remove the brownish epidermis from the lower end of a cutting, say for about two or three inches. It may easily be done, after the cutting has been kept in water several days previous. It is so hard that the young roots penetrate it with difficulty. Also the remaining parts of the bases of the foot stalks of the leaves ought to be scraped off; for fungoid growths destructive to the eyes above them form there easily.

In some parts of Germany, for instance, near *Heilbronn* on the *Neckar*, the cuttings, tied in bundles of about fifty or a hundred, several weeks previous to planting, are buried in the ground, but in an inverted position, that is, their tops downwards and their cut ends upwards. They are then covered with moss and soil, four or five inches deep, in a very sunny exposure, and kept moist. When taken out, most of them will be found rooted.

From *Dubreuil's* work, *Culture perfectionée, etc., du vignoble*, Paris, 1863, pp. 30 and 31, it appears that the vine cuttings are not unfrequently so treated in France. I called the attention of those interested to this process. (See Horticulturist, 1864, pp. 61, 62, 140 and 141).

Mr. Wm. Patrick, nurseryman at Terre Haute, Ind., has very much improved it. After a short notice, given in the Gardener's Monthly, he has furnished a full account of his method to the *Horticultural Annual*, published by Orange Judd & Co., 1867, from which I make an extract:

"Before the ground freezes, the cuttings, from four to six inches long, are tied in bundles of about fifty each, and the lower ends puddled by dipping them half their length in mud, made of loamy soil, mixed with water to about the consistency of cream. They are then, *lower ends down*, put in cold frames, fine soil is sprinkled over them to fill the spaces between the bundles, and they are then covered about four inches deep with earth. After they have been rained upon, and it begins to freeze, they are covered with leaves or straw, and sheltered by boards.

"In the spring, the mulch having been removed, sashes are laid on, but so that enough ventilation is provided; water is given, when needed, and so they root in about five weeks.

" Without sashes they will root, likewise, when treated in the manner just described. In this case they must be buried in an exposure inclined to the south. Should no roots have started in some of the cuttings, two pieces of bark, two or three inches long, on opposite sides of the lower ends of the cuttings, are taken off with a sharp knife. Treated and planted in this way, they make excellent plants. Cuttings of single eyes can be made to grow in the same way just as easily as longer cuttings.

"This plan is especially adapted to cuttings from the Delaware and other hard-wooded varieties."

Diel says in his well known and highly valued work, " Fruit Trees in Pots," third edition, Frankfort-on-the-Main, 1804, p. 212. " We had *never* succeeded in raising Paradise stocks for dwarfing the apple, from cuttings. By treating such cuttings as described in the above, I am raising hundreds of them every year. I keep the cuttings in sand during the winter, and bury them, in the spring, as soon as the frost is fairly out of the ground, in a sunny spot, the top ends downwards, and cover their lower ends, (which are, of course, up,) with moss three or four inches deep, sprinkling them, when needed, with lukewarm water. This method is applicable in raising plants from a number of shrubs and trees. As it is not generally known or practiced, I deem it my duty to thoroughly recommend it."

CUTTINGS MADE OF SINGLE EYES.

They are made by cutting a cane into as many pieces as it has well developed eyes on perfectly ripe wood; when

5*

an inch and a half long, so that there is an inch of wood
below, and half an inch of wood above the bud, they are
of the right size. The cuts may be made by means of a
knife or of good garden shears, which are now so made
that they do not bruise, but make a clean cut.

The eyes, so prepared, ought to be put in water and
left there for ten or twelve hours. This will soften the
remnants of the base of the leaf-stalk, so that it may easily
be removed by scraping. If such cuttings can be made
during the months of January and February, it is advisable to pack them in moist, not wet, moss or sand, and to
keep them there, free from frost, till wanted for planting.
Hard wood varieties, especially the *Delaware*, grow with
certainty from single eye cuttings treated in this way.

Cuttings of single eyes do not grow very easily in the
open air, when planted in beds; either frames with a
gentle heat must be prepared for them, or a propagating
bench in a green-house must be arranged for them.
Although a tank, connected with a heating boiler, in which
water, heated by the boiler, circulates, is, beyond question,
the best arrangement, yet a common flue, enclosed by
two brick walls, three feet distant from each other, and
covered by the propagating boxes, answers a very good
purpose. The bottom of these boxes consists of slate or
tin, resting on cross-strips, extending from one side-board
to the other. If these side-boards are from eight to nine
inches wide, and if the boxes are filled with washed sand
to the depth of four inches, there is room enough for the
young plants to develop and grow sufficiently, before they
are planted out. The distance of the bottom of the boxes
from the flue must, of course, be so regulated, that the
heat reaching the bottom shall not be too great. As
such flues generally rise a little along their whole length,
the top of the flue, near its inlet, is further removed from
the bottom of the flue, than towards it outlet. The boxes,
being level, are, therefore, nearer to the flue towards its

outlet, than at the beginning. Besides, flat stones or bricks may be laid on the flue near the fire-place, and two openings ought to be made in the inside wall, closed with shutters. In this way the temperature derived may easily be regulated and maintained.

To cover the propagating boxes either with sashes, or calico or paper frames, is a very good plan to regulate the moisture and to shade the cuttings.

The cuttings are planted immediately in the sand, or in pots plunged into it. Some set them straight, others in a slanting position, but, at all events, deep enough to have the eye just at a level with the sand, or covered about a quarter or half an inch by it. Many lay them horizontally on the sand, pack them on, and cover them about a quarter or half an inch deep with it. There exists also a difference of opinion in regard to the form of the cuttings; but the method, detailed in the above, is certain in its results, provided the right temperature and a proper degree of moisture are provided.

The principle of the proper treatment of such cuttings is based on the laws of vegetable physiology. It is contained in the following : *In order to facilitate the emission of roots, the lower ends of the cuttings must be kept during a certain period in a temperature that is several degrees higher than that which surrounds their tops.* At the outset, a temperature of from forty to fifty degrees is sufficient ; this is to be raised gradually to seventy-five or eighty, still later, even to ninety degrees when the cuttings grow vigorously and are well rooted. In general, it is much better not to increase the bottom heat too much. At the time when the cuttings are placed in the sand, it is not difficult to maintain a temperature in the house which is lower than that in the propagating boxes ; later, a higher temperature of the house has no deleterious effect.

As soon as the cuttings are placed in the sand, they must be thoroughly sprinkled with water, so that all the sand is moistened. The sand must never become too dry. When the cuttings are watered once a day, or in the beginning even less frequently, it is sufficient. The condition of the sand itself is a never failing guide in this simple operation. It is hardly necessary to caution here against the use of cold water. It must be warmed a little, either on the fire, or by adding hot water. As to the best time for planting cuttings, it is advisable not to be in too great haste. For long cuttings to be grown out of doors, the middle, or even the end, of April or the beginning of May is the time most suitable; for single eyes the beginning of March is best, although the process is often commenced very early in the winter. Long cuttings remain in the place where they are planted until fall or even until the spring following, but in this case under sufficient covering. They are then taken up and heeled-in, if this takes place in the fall, or planted where they are intended to grow. Those not sufficiently well rooted are planted in fertile soil, after their roots have been shortened a little, to grow there another season before they are planted in the places assigned to them.

Cuttings of one eye each are either taken out of the sand and planted in small pots, and frequently transplanted into larger ones, or into borders made in the open air, which is preferable. In the latter case furrows several inches deep are made, at the bottom of which the young plants are put, in little holes, so deep that the woody part of the cuttings is covered; the roots, which are very brittle, must not be injured, but spread evenly, so that they retain their natural position; then the hole is filled with water that is not too cold, and the holes are filled with fine soil before the water has time to sink in the ground.

The soil around the cuttings must not be pressed down, but they must be left in the condition in which water and soil placed them. To protect them during the first weeks by sashes, or calico frames, is deemed essential by some.

Others assert that when planted as described, they never suffer from the sun or the weather. I always shelter them for several weeks, and sprinkle them with water as often as required.

When they are growing vigorously, the soil is to be drawn towards their stems by filling up the furrows in which they have been planted.

It is astonishing to observe their growth when so planted and treated.

Last summer my cuttings made plants as thick as a goose quill, from twelve to fifteen feet long. I never tie them to sticks, but permit them to trail on the ground.

CUTTINGS FROM GREEN SHOOTS WITH A PIECE OF THE CANE (OLD WOOD) ATTACHED TO IT.

This form is intermediate between cuttings made of old wood and those made of green shoots. Such cuttings, even of hard wooded kinds like the Delaware, root very easily.

When the young shoots in May have attained the length of about four inches, they are cut off from the cane, so that about an inch or two inches of old wood below the shoot is preserved, and about half an inch above it. If the green shoots are a little too long, their tops must be removed. They are then so planted in sand that the old wood lies horizontally in it, and is covered half an inch or an inch deep.

The green shoots are then in an erect position. No bottom heat is required, though a little of it does not injure them. Nearly every one of the cuttings made in this way grows; they will be found rooted in a short time, and make very fine and vigorous plants. They are planted out and treated in precisely the same way as described in the above. I accidentally discovered this method of propagating vines several years ago. It was, however, known to others long before I discovered it, as Mr. P. B. Mead, the then Editor of the Horticulturist, informed me.

I described the plan several years ago in that magazine. (See 1864, p. 61, and 1865, pp. 140 and 141).

CUTTINGS MADE OF GREEN SHOOTS.

Such cuttings grow very easily, when managed in the right way. They are cut from the cane, and shortened to two or three buds, removing the leaves, except the uppermost. The lowest part of the shoot, being firmer and more solid than the upper part, is to be preferred; still even the upper part will, under proper management, grow. The cut, by which the cutting is severed from the cane, or from the shoot, must always be made below a bud. The bud may not be discernible at the base of the shoot; but if the shoot is cut off exactly at the place where it proceeds from the cane, along with a *very thin slice* of the latter, the cutting will be in the right condition. Sand is the best material for making such cuttings grow. A moderate bottom heat is very desirable, but not absolutely indispensable. Several years ago, I saw a large number of them grow on the propagating bench in one of the houses of my friends, the Messrs. Parsons, at Flushing. The house was kept very warm, but no bottom heat had been given.

It is of vital importance to regulate the watering with the greatest care; they must, of course, be shaded, when required, and the atmosphere around them must be kept damp, but not so damp as to cause their decay.

According to a communication from Mr. Pr. Rubens, (author of a valuable work on the culture of the vine,) in a letter to me, cuttings of green shoots about 18 inches long, when planted during the summer in holes a foot deep, will grow in the open air.

When well rooted, such cuttings are treated in precisely the same way as others. In order to make them strong plants, they must be transplanted several times, that is, in successive years, shortening their roots a little each time.

The question has often been discussed, which kind of cuttings makes the best plants. From the experience of intelligent and skillful cultivators of the vine, it appears now to be an established fact, that good plants may, under a suitable treatment, be obtained, whatever method may be used. Cuttings, however, made of single eyes, are generally considered the best; they unite, indeed, so many advantages in them, that I do not hesitate to recommend them as preferable.

III.—BY GRAFTING.

The term *grafting* we use here in its broadest sense, including, like the French word *greffe*, not only grafting proper, but also inarching, budding, etc.

Common cleft grafting is performed in the usual way, either in March or April, or in May after two or three leaves are expanded on the stock, because the vine does not then bleed any more. It may be done below ground, which insures better success, or above ground, which is, if possible, to be avoided.

The stock is to be cut off horizontally below the ground, first removing the soil, pared smooth, and split. The scion, which must be in a dormant state, is cut to two eyes, the lower one of which must be just above the cut, after the wedge-shaped part of it has been inserted in the cleft, and carefully adjusted. If the stock is thick enough, no tying is required; the application of grafting wax is recommended by some, but cautioned against by others. The soil is then replaced and heaped up a little, in order to cover the upper eye about a quarter of an inch deep with soil. As in cuttings, the scion must not be cut off too close above the upper eye ; a piece, an inch long, must be left.

Mr. Andrew S. Fuller prefers the fall as the best season for grafting. The scion must, in this case, be protected from the frost by covering it with a flower-pot, earth and straw, which are to be removed as soon as the frost is fairly out of the ground.

Grafting is of little use, except under particular circumstances, and failures are so common, that it never will be generally adopted as a means of propagating the vine. It is asserted by Dr. Stayman, of Kansas, a scientific viticulturist, that taking off the bark from the stock, as well as from the scion, as far as the latter is inserted into the former, and not splitting the stock through to the opposite side, renders success certain.

Pieces of succulent roots six or eight inches long, dug towards the end of March and in the beginning of April, are very convenient for grafting. They ought to be so selected and cut, that each of them has some fibrous roots. They may be either cleft or splice grafted, tied firmly with worsted or other elastic woolen yarn, and kept in sand until the weather gets warm, that is, about the middle of April, when they may be planted at once in the garden. I always cover the horizontal cuts of them, when they are cleft grafted, with a little liquid grafting wax. Although scions with one eye will grow, yet I prefer greatly such as have two eyes, and plant the root grafts, if necessary on account of their length, in a slanting position, but *never too shallow.* The uppermost eye should touch the ground; it should be covered a little either with soil, sand, or moss.

We shall not devote any more space here to describing more artificial and complicated modes of grafting, nor shall we recommend budding in a peculiar way, as practised occasionally by some amateurs.

Grafting grapes below ground and root grafting have the disadvantage in common that the scions *throw out roots of their own.* However desirable this may be in vigorous growers and hardy kinds, yet if the scions are taken from kinds having weak and feeble roots, such roots, emitted by the scions, will unfailingly impart feebleness to the plant, and paralyze the strengthening influence of the stock.

INARCHING GREEN SHOOTS INTO GREEN SHOOTS OF GROWING STOCKS.

Last summer I had the good fortune of making the acquaintance of Dr. Charles Kenworthy, a gentleman recently from Australia. An enthusiastic amateur, and a close and keen observer, he, in almost daily conversations with me about scientific and practical viticulture, called my attention again to propagating the vine by green shoots, inarched into the green shoots of a growing vine. Years ago, I had, with success, grafted pieces of green shoots into the green shoots of growing vines, as stated and described in the Horticulturist, 1862, pp. 14 to 17, but as the procedure is rather too slow for this fast going country, I did not expect that any advantage would be derived from it. Otherwise it is similar in its effects to inarching, in making the vine dependent on the roots of the stock exclusively.

Inarching green shoots into green shoots is equally successful under glass and in the open air. The two vines to be united must be near enough to each other to effect the union. The stronger and the more vigorous the shoots · the better. A little of the bark and the underlying green substance of them is removed about an inch or an inch and a half long, and both are then tongued their whole length, the vine to be propagated, from *below upwards*, the stock, *from above downwards*. As the young shoots are very brittle, two persons are needed to perform the operation, one of them holding and steadying the vine tongued, the other operating upon the other, and uniting them. The tongue of the stock must go *from below upwards* into the tongued place of the other. Both are then tied rather firmly with oiled silk, on which a few grape leaves are put or folded together to keep the wounds cool and protect it from the influence of the direct rays of the sun.

About a fortnight after the operation, the stock must be cut off an inch or so above the junction; a week later, a cut is made into the vine to be propagated; this is made deeper, a few days later, and the vine is cut entirely off as soon as the union is complete. Then the leaves and the worsted are removed also. It is easy enough to determine, by occasionally examining the vines, so united, the proper time for the several steps to be taken. Eight experiments, made in my grounds under glass or in the open air, proved to be eight successes, although it was not only too late in the season when they were made, but the stocks as well as the other vines were growing poorly. Some of them were not thicker than a middle-sized knitting needle; consequently they could not be tongued, but were only wounded and tied together. The union in all of them is perfect; after the lapse of a year or two it will be impossible to distinguish it.

If it is true, as I believe from actual experience, that the cause of the failure of many kinds *lies in the root*, inarching will be a means of making feeble growing vines strong; perhaps even some of the hardier foreigners may, in this way, be inured to our changeable climate. It is impossible for me to make, in the course of this spring and summer, as many and as extensive experiments as I intended; still, from what I *know* already, I am confident of great advantages to be derived from this process. We would bring this method of propagation to the attention of horticulturists, feeling that it has heretofore been unduly neglected.

IV.—BY SEEDS.

As no plant is more apt to sport than the vine, when grown from the seed, this method of propagation must be resorted to in order to raise varieties different from those already in existence.

The best and ripest berries are selected, and either immediately planted, whole, about half an inch or an inch deep, and protected by leaves, moss, or straw, from too severe freezing, or they may be dried without artificial heat, and the seeds may be taken out in the spring and planted. The plan adopted by me is, to separate the seeds from the pulp, as soon as the berries are ripe, and to plant them in pots, filled with light, but fertile soil, which I keep during the winter in the cellar, sprinkling several times with a little water. In the month of March following I place the pots in a window of a warm room, or plunge them in a hot or propagating bed, watering them regularly. The seeds, separated from the pulp, may also be kept in papers and planted in the following spring in pots or in the open air. To shade the young plants a little, when they are growing in the open air, is very beneficial. A. S. Fuller sows, for this purpose, apple seeds along with the grape seeds, or in a row, immediately before them to the south. The young apple trees do not make many fibrous roots the first year; they do not, therefore, interfere with the vines, but afford them shade, and, in a measure, support. That the young plants must be watered in dry weather, and that they must be kept clean, need not expressly be recommended.

In the autumn, after the fall of the leaf, they are to be taken up and heeled-in, which is more advisable than to cover them up, as the frost would heave them up more or

less, and would break many of their roots. In the spring
their roots are shortened a little, they are pruned down to
the lowest good bud, and planted in furrows several inches
deep. In the course of the summer the furrows are filled
up. The young plants are then treated exactly like other
young vines. They will bear in the fifth year, but some
of them will do so in the third or fourth, others in the sixth
or seventh years.

When whole berries are planted, young plants will come
up, not only in the first spring after planting, but also in
the second and third, as stated by Mr. E. Bull, of Concord, Mass., the originator of the Concord. Therefore,
in lifting young plants grown from planting whole berries in the first fall, care should be taken to disturb the
soil as little as possible.

The process of raising vines from seed is very tedious,
and unsatisfactory in its results. The seeds from American varieties produce a large proportion of male (stami-
nate) plants; they often are, and that is the rule, inferior
to the parent. In five thousand seedlings, raised at one
time by Dr. Grant, there were but two worthy to be preserved, the *Iona* and the *Israella*. Among five hundred
seedlings from the *Isabella* which I have grown, there is
but *one* better than the mother plant. A most excellent
white grape from a seed of a Crimean grape, which is perfectly hardy and vigorous in my grounds, is the result from
planting but two seeds. This is, however, so rare an accident that it may not happen again in a century. A full
description of the grape in question is given by me in the
Gardener's Monthly, 1866, pp. 291 and 292. The plant
and the fruit have been carefully examined by many con-
noisseurs and experienced vine-growers. They all unite in
the belief that the vine is thoroughly healthy and vigorous,
and "*that the fruit is most excellent*," to use the words of
the Agriculturist in an editorial notice of it. See Agriculturist, 1866, p. 438.

HYBRIDIZATION.

There is a difference between *hybridization* and *crossing*, but as my object is not to enter here into scientific disquisitions, I will describe, as briefly as possible, the mode of the operation itself. Moreover we know that the species are not constant, but variable.

The petals (floral leaves) of a vine blossom are five in number, cohering and thrown off by the stamens when the blossom is expanding. They look then like a cap. The fine stamens bear on their summits the anthers, little bodies covered with a fine powder or dust, called pollen. While the petals are raised by the stamens, fructification frequently takes place before the petals are thrown off. This fructification is effected by the pollen, coming in contact with the upper end of the pistil. The pistil excretes a somewhat viscid matter on its upper end, to which the dust of the pollen adheres. It is then carried down into the ovarium, the lower part of the pistil. In this way fructification is accomplished. A small berry is formed which enlarges daily until it attains its proper size. A blossom not impregnated by the pollen, does not develop itself; it remains diminutive.

To prevent natural fructification the blossoms must be carefully watched. As soon as some of them have opened on a certain cluster selected for artificial fructification, they are cut off with scissors, together with a number of the remaining buds to diminish the number. This not only facilitates the operation, but tends to develop those remaining much better. The petals of the buds left are then examined with a needle; they are lifted and removed. Should they not yield, they must remain undisturbed for an hour, or long enough for their removal. Should any blossoms expand during the absence of the operator, they must be carefully cut off, lest some of the pollen of their stamens might reach the pistils of other blossoms already

operated upon, thus rendering the experiment uncertain
and unreliable.

Pollen of the species or variety to be used for the male,
is then taken up by means of a fine camels-hair painter's
brush, and dusted by shaking or gently tapping the handle
of the brush. This must be repeated several times on the
same blossom. If the first operation was performed in
the forenoon, it ought to be repeated in the afternoon.
Calm and warm weather is most favorable for this work.
To enclose the clusters with thin gauze to prevent the in-
terference of insects and wind, until the berries begin to
swell, is certainly a very good plan.

It is not often the case that the species or varieties,
intended for hybridization, blossom at the same time, but
the plant to be used as the male parent usually blooms
earlier than the other. Some pollen is then shaken from a
cluster, it being in the right condition, upon a piece of paper, and preserved in a tightly corked phial until wanted.
Dubreuil asserts that pollen from some plants, preserved
between two watch glasses, united and glued together by
means of small pieces of paper, will not lose its vital
power in the course of a whole year. I do not think,
however, that watch glasses are any better than tightly
corked and sealed phials. Mr. Hovey, of Cambridge,
Mass., fertilized his lily, *Melpomene,* with pollen from the
auratum, when it bloomed for the first time in England,
and obtained crosses which were in bloom last summer,
showing unmistakably that hybridization had been accomplished. That the pollen from vines remains good for a
month, I know from actual experiments, and I do not
doubt in the least that it will keep much longer.

Hybridization offers a wide field for improving our native kinds. As yet, our best grapes are chance seedlings;
still the experiments made by Messrs. Allen, Moore and
Caywood, are encouraging, though effective hybridization
is doubted by many. The criterion of Mr. A. S. Fuller is

a very good one, indeed, viz. : *To sow the seeds from a plant claimed to be a hybrid, and to ascertain whether the young plants sport much, some showing the characteristics of the father, others those of the mother. Should they all be similar to each other, the probability would be that hybridization had not been effected.*

Two years ago, I called the attention of my friend, Dr. Thurber, the scientific botanist, to eleven seedlings from Allen's Hybrid. They are so much alike, and so similar in their relation to the parent, that he was very much astonished at the fact before him. On the other hand, of the five hundred seedlings from the Isabella, raised by me, no two were alike in regard to lobation, growth, etc.

Be this as it may, experiments in this direction ought to be continued with assiduity and zeal ; results will ultimately be reached, that will benefit the country in a high degree.

Here I will mention, in conclusion, that Naumann's Cibebe, the most beautiful of all grapes in form, is the product of an intentional, artificial crossing of the large yellow from Smyrna and the Muscat Schwarz-Welscher, obtained by the great ornithologist, Naumann, late Professor in the University of Leipsic. Mr. Neubert, of that city, made me a present of it.

HINTS ON THE GENERAL MANAGEMENT OF AMERICAN SPECIES AND VARIETIES.

I.—PLANTING.

For planting, the fall is preferred by many, the spring by others. To protect the vines, regularly planted in the fall, from freezing and thawing during the winter, as well as from the water accumulating in the holes and forming ice in them, is much more difficult than to heel them in, and to preserve them in this way. On the other hand, there is so much work to be done in the spring, that there is danger of hastening the planting too much, although this process is so important that it is impossible to do it too carefully. No mistake, made in planting, can afterwards be corrected.

I have made many experiments, and have met with so many failures and disappointments from fall planting in this latitude, that I *buy* such vines as I intend to try in the fall, but I always plant them in the spring. *Buying* in the fall is advisable, as a better selection can be made, but *planting* in the spring is surer of success.

Heeling-in is an operation so well known, that I need not describe it here. Should the ground be stiff and heavy, it is much better to lay the plants against a little mound in a slanting position on the surface of the earth than in a ditch, in which the water would collect during the winter. Sand or fine soil ought to be used for filling in among the roots. This must be done so carefully that even the smallest rootlet is embedded in, and covered by, the sand or soil; for mould will grow on roots not packed firmly in sand or soil. Soil may be used for increasing the thickness of the mound, covering the roots, and some boards may be placed on the top of it to carry off the rain water, and to prevent the sun from warming the plants, so heeled in, too much. As the frost acts *horizontally* also—to speak not scientifically, but practically—the covering ought to extend about two feet beyond the ends of the roots. In heeling-in I always cover the whole plants, roots and all.

Vines keep very well in boxes, filled with sand, that are placed in the cellar, or they may be covered with sand in the cellar without boxes.

Spring planting ought to be deferred till air and soil are sufficiently warmed, that is, from the middle to the end of April. Should the buds have commenced showing life again, it is so much the better.

The roots of the plants must be carefully examined, in order to cut off such as are bruised or broken. To shorten them a little, to have fresh cuts on all of them, is judicious, but to remove one-half or two-thirds of them, involves an injurious waste of strength. Finally, the vines must be cut down to the lowest well-developed bud. There is *then* no danger arising from bleeding.

The holes for the plants ought to be large enough for the reception of the roots in their natural position, and about a foot deep. Then some fine soil is heaped up in the middle of each; resembling a mole heap, but more pointed and conical. On the top of this heap the young plant is placed, and its roots are spread out evenly, and properly arranged for making them grow in all directions. Fine soil is then sprinkled or sifted on them until they are well covered. Then some water must be poured on through the rose of a watering-pot, that the soil may settle, and the holes fill with soil, leaving a space of about four inches open during the summer. Rain showers will carry some soil into them, and fill them up partially, which is not injurious to the growth of the young plants. In the fall some more soil must be added to make them level.

The roots ought to be four or six inches below the ground, at least deep enough not to be injured by hoeing, digging, or plowing, but not too deep, as it is customary with some. The depth to which the soil is to be worked afterward is the surest guide ; *the roots should, under all circumstances, be beyond the reach of the implements to be used.* If the vines are to be layered during one or more successive years, to furnish them with more roots, they must not be planted in an *erect*, but in an *inclined* position, (at an angle of about 45°), otherwise it is not unfrequently difficult to bend them down and to lay them in a ditch, made for this purpose.

The management of plants having more than one tier of roots, or of such as are older, does not differ in princi-

6

ple from that of young plants. Its modification, according
to circumstances, will be obvious to any one intending to
plant them. The long, woody roots of old vines must be
very severely pruned; they ought to be cut off below a
thin succulent root, proceeding from them, and the cut
ought to be made at its *underside*, so that the wound may
be pressed on the soil below. If cut at *the upperside*, it
will be apt to decay from the water falling or trickling
down upon it.

The plan of mulching vines, recently planted, is a good
one ; to manure, however, the soil below or about their
roots cannot be too strongly denounced as injurious and
dangerous in the highest degree. Many vines are killed
every year, or ruined beyond the possibility of recovery,
by well-meaning, but inexperienced persons. While they
would withhold fat pork or beef from a patient when con-
valescent, and yet feeble in consequence of a severe shock,
to which their health was exposed, they do not hesitate to
treat a vine, in a similar condition, with a superabundance
of heavy, indigestible food. Can anything be more incon-
sistent ?

II.—PRUNING.

The principles of pruning as practised in Europe, and
so lucidly explained by *Dr. Mohr*, are undoubtedly correct. Still, even in Europe, different countries require
modifications in the application of them. This is also the
case in the United States. The climate is warm during
the summer; we have twice as much rain as in France,
and much more when we compare the quantity of rain
which falls here, with that which is received in California,
where the temperature is very high. Then again, we have
severe droughts with so small an amount of water in the
air, that it is almost incredible. See the thoroughly scientific observations of *J. S. Lippincott*, Esq., in the Report of the Commissioner of Agriculture, 1863, pp. 520-

550. His Vapor Index, for sale by *J. W. Queen*, 924 Chestnut street, Philadelphia, is a most ingenious and convenient instrument for ascertaining at a glance the amount of aqueous vapor in the atmosphere, or in a room, provided a wet bulb thermometer in connection with a dry bulb thermometer can be consulted.

The conditions of our climate favor a rampant wood-growth; consequently we must not prune too short to insure the health of the vine, and to obtain abundant crops.

There is another consideration of vital importance, to which I wish to call the attention of every horticulturist most earnestly. *It lies in the fact that some kinds have their Fruit shoots on the upper part of the cane, others on the lower part.* My friend, *Wm. Saunders*, Esq., the eminently able Superintendent of the Experimental Garden at Washington, cautions, on p. 15 of the Agricultural Report of 1865, against the close pruning of such rampant growers as the *Clinton, Taylor, Alvey, Franklin, etc.,* asserting that they will bear profusely when but slightly pruned back; otherwise a mass of wood will be produced. This was incontrovertibly proven on my grounds last year. An *Alvey* that had borne abundantly the year previous, was pruned too close by a friend of mine, a skillful and experienced viticulturist. The result was exactly in accordance with Mr. Saunders' statement; the vine in question, which was loaded with fruit the year previous, bore not more than half-a-dozen clusters last year.

It is not always without danger to recommend a single modification of the pruning principle as applicable to every variety. We know that certain kinds of the apple, pear, etc., require different treatment in this respect; how could it be expected, then, that all kinds of the vine should be alike?

What is most needed, therefore, is, to ascertain whether the lower buds of the canes of certain varieties produce bearing shoots, or those more distant from the bases of the canes.   The true method of pruning them will be the result, so much desired.

George Husmann, Esq., of *Hermann, Missouri*, discovered accidentally that the laterals of the Concord and other strong growing varieties, when pruned in the fall to four or six buds, produce the finest clusters and the most abundant crops to be obtained.   This took place in 1862. *See the Cultivation of the Native Grape, by George Husmann*, p. 61.   Since then he has adopted it altogether for such varieties as mentioned, with the most satisfactory result.   He suffers the shoots intended for bearing canes to grow about four feet high, and then removes their tops by pinching.   He retains four or five laterals, which he prunes, in the fall, to four or six buds.

This is important ; experiments should be made to ascertain accurately the varieties most adapted to this mode of treatment, and the localities favorable to it.

The correctness of Mr. *Husmann's* observations is corroborated by the results of similar experiments intentionally made in Germany, as early as 1857.   They are mentioned and described by Dr. *E. Lucas*, the celebrated scientific and practical Pomologist and Director of the Pomological Institute at *Reuttingen*, in the Kingdom of *Wurtemberg*.   In his *Annual for Pomologists, Gardeners*, etc., published in 1860, from pp. 59-61, he gives a detailed description of the successful experiments of Mr. *Deuringer*, of *Sendling*, near *Munich*, in *Bavaria*; they are exactly like those made by Mr. *Husmann*, except that Mr. *Deuringer* suffered the shoots intended for canes to grow five or six feet high before he stopped them, in order to excite the growth of the laterals.

Mr. *Deuringer's* experiments are based on reasoning concerning the proper function of the laterals; he *invented* his method, while Mr. Husmann *discovered* it.

Mr. *Husmann's* personal character is so well known, and deservedly stands so high, that I am very far from attempting to insinuate that he was acquainted with Mr. *Dæuringer's* operations. The Annual is so rare, that it may be doubtful whether there exists another copy of it in the United States than the one in my possession. The coincidence goes only to show how difficult it is in horticulture to add anything not already known to somebody else to the stock of facts.

Young plants must, at the fall pruning, be cut down to the lowest well-developed bud, that is, to the first, second, or third. During the first summer they must not be tied to stakes, nor pinched. When trailing on the ground or climbing over some brushwood placed near them, the upper tendency of the sap, common to most plants, and especially strong in the vine, is, in a measure, counteracted, by which the root is very much strengthened. Also in the second year I treat them in this way. The treatment of older vines must be the same as that of plants but one year old.

Before the vines attain the thickness of a finger, they must not be pruned long for bearing, but must be cut down in every successive fall.

III.—PINCHING.

The shoots for bearing canes must not be pinched or stopped at all during their growth, and their laterals must be permitted to develop at will. In regard to the bearing shoots, it is doubtful to me whether close pinching, that is, beyond, or at the third leaf from the last cluster, is advantageous in this country or not. Apart from the practice, growing more into favor every day, according to which the shoots are left longer, and are, perhaps, pinched but once during the season, I am free to confess that I have done so much orthodox pinching, but with results so little satisfactory to my expectation, that I feel strongly inclined to indulge in a little greater latitude in this respect than formerly. Experiments, instituted on purpose, and varied as to varieties, sorts, and localities, are very much needed; they will enable us to arrive at the true method.

That the laterals of young plants, or of older ones transplanted, must not be pinched, has already been observed in the above.

IV.—COVERING IN THE FALL, AND LIFTING IN THE FOLLOWING SPRING.

In this extreme climate it is reasonable to lay the vines down on the ground and to cover them, especially such kinds as are tender. Still, all kinds are benefited by this process.

Sand or sandy soil is a good material for covering; stiff clay is objectionable. On the sand, flat stones are placed to keep the vines in place.

Some use straw, manure, sods, and stones, without soil or sand, for covering; these materials, however, ought to be avoided. They leave everywhere empty spaces, in which mice find shelter. Mice are pests in a plantation of vines. Manure is apt to ferment, by which process the vines may be excited to a premature growth under the cover, and consequently they may greatly suffer or even perish.

A very good covering material is dust (refuse) of hard (Anthracite) coal. I have used it for a number of years with decided benefit, so that I shall not use anything else for the future. No mould is formed on the vines, so covered, nor do mice or other animals harbor in it.

As soon as the frost is fairly out of the ground in the Spring, that is, in the first weeks of April, the vines must be freed from their covering and left for a certain time to swing in the air, before they are tied to their poles or trellises.

The rule ought never to be lost sight of, neither to cover too early, that is, not before the soil is frozen, nor to lift too early.

Sheltering the vines by boards nailed on the top of the

trellis posts tends to protect them against the attacks of mildew, according to Mr. Saunders' experience. Such partial roofs render radiation beneath them impossible, so that the vines, as well as the soil, remain warmer than without protection. Dr. *Schroeder*, of *Bloomington, Illinois*, mulches his vines four or six inches deep with straw, after they had ceased blossoming. Vines, so treated, were free from mildew, and the grapes did not rot.

I might devote here some space to insects and other animals, injurious to the vine; but as I could hardly do more than repeat what is found in many books, I forego it. The chief remedy lies in the hand of the vine grower; thrips yield only to the application of sulphur.

AMERICAN VARIETIES.

It would not only be almost impossible, but also useless, to give here a complete list of native grapes; both the amateur and the professional grape grower will resort to other sources for their information on this point, not to *this* book. We mention here only the most valuable kinds, nearly all of which we have tested in our own grounds, following chiefly the American Horticultural Annual for 1867, without even changing the wording of many descriptions: for they are very concise and characteristic.

Adirondac.—Black. A good and healthy grower in our grounds. Fruit very fine, sweet and luscious.

Allen's Hybrid.—White. Tolerably healthy with us, sweet and vinous.

Alvey.—Black. A vigorous, healthy grower; suffers very little from mildew; juice colored; skin exceedingly thin; without pulp. Ripens in September. It improves very much by hanging long on the vine, from which it never drops. Vinous, sprightly and refreshing.

Anna.—White. A poor bearer and grower with us. High flavored, tough pulp.

Catawba.—Red. Too well known to need description. Is doing well in our grounds.

Clinton.—Black. A healthy, rampant grower. Colors long before it is ripe. Not fit for the table, but good for wine.

Concord.—Black. Known as the grape for the million.

Creveling.—Black. Good healthy grower. Hardy and very early. Cluster loose. Very valuable.

Delaware.—Red. Delicious. A good, not a rampant grower. Hardy, but mildews in some localities.

Diana.—Red. Does very well with us, but is not to be depended upon in some localities. High flavored and sweet. Skin very thick. Keeps well.

Diana Hamburg.—Black. A delicious grape, but said to be late.

Elsinburg.—Black. Very fine and hardy grape. Very small, clusters large.

Hartford Prolific.—Black. Very early, vigorous, hardy. Sweet, tough, acid pulp. Drops from the peduncle.

Herbemont.—Black. Very small, clusters large; vinous and excellent, but late.

Iona.—Red. Healthy in many localities, in others it suffers from mildew. Fruit praised in every respect for table and wine.

Isabella.—Black. Known everywhere. Very variable and uncertain.

Israella.—Black. Good and early grape.

Ives' Seedling.—Black. Highly praised for wine.

Lydia.—White. Hardy and early; promises very well.

Martha.—White. A white Concord, but sweeter. Very vigorous and healthy.

Maxatawney.—White. Vigorous and healthy, but late. When thoroughly ripe it is a fine grape.

Miles.—Black. Very early and better than Hartford Prolific.

Norton's Virginia.—Black. Known and praised as the best grape for red wine.

Rebecca.—White. Very fine, but a poor grower on its own roots. Should be grafted on the roots of some vigorous variety.

Rogers' Hybrids.—Black, red, and amber. Most of them vigorous growers and healthy. Berries and clusters in some of them very large and fine. The following are known as very valuable: Nos. 1, 2, 3, 4, 5, 9, 15, 19, 22, 30, 33, 43, 44.

To Kalon.—Black. Healthy with us, but a poor bearer; excellent.

Union Village.—Black. Very large and showy.; of fair quality. A good grower with us.

Walter.—Red. Very sweet and high flavored; very early.

Weehawken.—White. A most remarkable seedling of ours, raised from a seed of a Crimean variety, imported by us. The most healthy of all our vines. Cluster beautiful; vinous, high flavored. Never mildewed. Not yet disseminated.

THE

GRAPE CULTURIST,

BY

ANDREW S. FULLER.

NEW AND ENLARGED EDITION.

THE STANDARD WORK

ON THE CULTIVATION OF THE HARDY GRAPE,
AS IT NOT ONLY DISCUSSES PRINCIPLES,
BUT

· **ILLUSTRATES PRACTICE.**

Every thing is made perfectly plain, and its teachings may be followed upon

ONE VINE OR A VINEYARD.

The following are some of the topics that are treated:

GROWING NEW VARIETIES FROM SEED.
PROPAGATION BY SINGLE BUDS OR EYES.
PROPAGATING HOUSES AND THEIR MANAGEMENT FULLY DESCRIBED.
HOW TO GROW.
CUTTINGS IN OPEN AIR, AND HOW TO MAKE LAYERS.
GRAFTING THE GRAPE—A SIMPLE AND SUCCESSFUL METHOD.
HYBRIDIZING AND CROSSING—MODE OF OPERATION.
SOIL AND SITUATION—PLANTING AND CULTIVATION.
PRUNING, TRAINING, AND TRELLISES—ALL THE SYSTEMS EXPLAINED
GARDEN CULTURE—HOW TO GROW VINES IN A DOOR-YARD.
INSECTS, MILDEW, SUN-SCALD, AND OTHER TROUBLES.
DESCRIPTION OF THE VALUABLE AND THE DISCARDED VARIETIES.

Sent post-paid.   Price $1.50.

Orange Judd & Co., 41 Park Row.

T H E

SMALL FRUIT CULTURIST.

BY

ANDREW S. FULLER.

Beautifully Illustrated.

We have heretofore had no work especially devoted to small fruits, and certainly no treatises anywhere that give the information contained in this. It is to the advantage of special works that the author can say all that he has to say on any subject, and not be restricted as to space, as he must be in those works that cover the culture of all fruits—great and small.

This book covers the whole ground of Propagating Small Fruits, their Culture, Varieties, Packing for Market, etc. While very full on the other fruits, the Currants and Raspberries have been more carefully elaborated than ever before, and in this important part of his book, the author has had the invaluable counsel of Charles Downing. The chapter on gathering and packing the fruit is a valuable one, and in it are figured all the baskets and boxes now in common use. The book is very finely and thoroughly illustrated, and makes an admirable companion to the Grape Culturist, by the same author.

———◆———

CONTENTS:

———

Sent post-paid.   Price $1.50.   .

———

ORANGE JUDD & CO., 41 PARK ROW.

www.ingramcontent.com/pod-product-compliance
Lightning Source LLC
Chambersburg PA
CBHW030612270326
41927CB00007B/1143